BASS
FRETBOARD WORKBOOK

Essential Music Principles and Concepts
for Fretboard Mastery

by Chad Johnson

ISBN 978-1-4584-1619-3

HAL•LEONARD®
CORPORATION

7777 W. BLUEMOUND RD. P.O. BOX 13819 MILWAUKEE, WI 53213

In Australia Contact:
Hal Leonard Australia Pty. Ltd.
4 Lentara Court
Cheltenham, Victoria, 3192 Australia
Email: ausadmin@halleonard.com.au

Visit Hal Leonard Online at
www.halleonard.com

TABLE OF CONTENTS

INTRODUCTION

Welcome to *Bass Fretboard Workbook*. Get ready to flex your mind muscles and gain command of that unruly bass neck! The information contained here is applicable to all styles of bass playing and can be put to use immediately in practice and performance. If you're tired of getting frustrated at the sight of those daunting upper frets, then it's time to face your demons. This book is geared toward several different types of players:

- **Beginners**: Even if this is your first time picking up the instrument, you can gain a lot from this book. Although the issue of playing technique is not covered here, the information can be used as a companion guide while you study a more comprehensive playing method.

- **Intermediate Players**: Many intermediate level bassists have several years of playing under their belt and are quite adept technically but have neglected to learn the fretboard inside and out. This book will aid in fretboard memorization.

- **Advanced "Ear" Players:** Maybe you're an advanced player that can hang with the best of them once you've slid that finger up and down the neck to determine the key of a song. If so, this book will help rid you of that habit once and for all.

The applications for the knowledge you'll gain in this book are far-reaching to say the least. Here are a few of the rewards that come with sticking it out and working through this entire book:

- Your ability to communicate with other musicians will grow in leaps and bounds.

- You'll spend much less time learning songs.

- You'll feel more freedom when creating bass lines, both technically and creatively.

- Your understanding of harmony will improve.

- You'll no longer feel chained to one position throughout an entire song or riff.

Simply put, you'll improve as a bass player. There's no reason to shy away from learning the neck. It won't bite you, and it's not as difficult as it seems; I promise. So take a moment and look at the neck one last time, because the mysterious regions won't be so puzzling for long.

HOW TO USE THIS BOOK

This book starts at the very beginning and assumes that you know practically nothing about the bass neck—not even the names of the open strings. This may be below the level of many of you, but I encourage everyone to start from the beginning. The groundwork covered in the earlier chapters is built upon in latter ones, and you'll need to be thoroughly familiar with most of the early concepts and ideas in order to fully digest the new information.

For the more advanced among you, if you must skip ahead, do so, but please don't let the Table of Contents be your guide here. Skim through the early pages and make sure you're clear on everything covered. The moment you find something that's not second nature to you, stop there and start working forward.

You'll find that certain concepts will be easier to grasp than others. This is perfectly normal, and you should plan on spending more time on certain chapters than on others. With consistent practice of several sessions per week, you'll most likely work through this entire book within a few months. If you're not able to devote that much time or it takes longer than that, don't worry. Take all the time you need to get this information solid. The most important thing is that you actually possess the knowledge once finished. Rushing through the book in a week with no comprehension to show for it won't do any good at all. Slow and steady wins the race!

HOW TO READ THE DIAGRAMS

Throughout this book, scale diagrams or grids are used to indicate notes on the fretboard. If you're not familiar with this type of notation, you'll need to understand it before you proceed.

The four horizontal lines represent the strings of the bass. The lowest pitched or thickest string is at the bottom of the diagram, and the highest pitched or thinnest string is at the top. The vertical lines represent the frets. This is the same point of view as when you glance down at the fretboard (you may have to bend forward a bit) while the bass is in playing position.

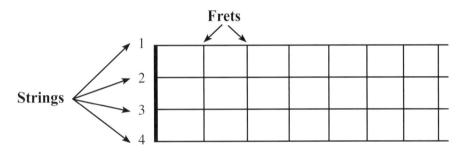

Sometimes, the nut is shown on the far left side, and the fret numbers are indicated along the top, marking the frets that commonly have inlays (third, fifth, seventh, etc.).

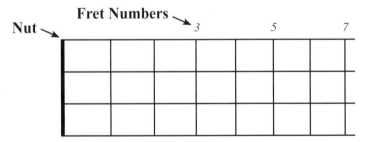

Other times, a smaller portion of the fretboard is shown. In these instances, when the nut is not shown, the first fret will have a fret marker indicating the position. In all diagrams, the notes to play are shown as circles—either hollow or solid, depending on the note (this will be explained later).

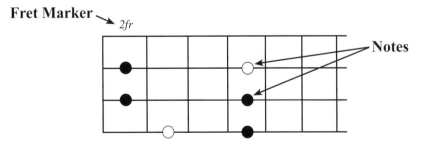

CHAPTER 1:
EACH STRING IS A MINI-PIANO (That Can Only Play One Note at a Time)

Many players see the bass neck as a mysterious collection of lines and dots—connected one way at certain times, other ways at different times, and disconnected completely at other times. In this way, it's almost like a switchboard in a constant state of flux. Our first step in taking command of the bass fretboard starts with realizing that this is not the case at all. There is order to this apparent chaos, and we'll begin looking at one string at a time. After all, **each string is a mini-piano that can only play one note at a time**.

So what do we mean by this? A bass string doesn't look or sound much like a piano. And it certainly doesn't weigh as much as one. When it comes to pitch layout, however, it's incredibly similar. It comes down to this: **Each fret on a bass string corresponds to one key on the piano.**

This simple fact is essential knowledge with regards to understanding more complex musical concepts like intervals and scales. Regardless of how complicated something seems, you can always reduce it to this one-string mini-piano approach. Let's get to it and see what I mean.

THE OPEN STRINGS
In case you've managed to avoid it thus far, you simply must learn the names of the open strings before we can get anywhere. It'll be painless, I promise, and it'll be much easier than memorizing the state capitals.

LOW IS HIGH AND TOP IS BOTTOM?
I see a lot of players confused with this, so we need to address it right away. Throughout this book, we'll be using terms such as "bottom," "top," "lower," "higher," etc. It's very important to realize that these terms nearly always refer to **pitch**—i.e., higher or lower sounds—and *not* physical space. This means that, even though it's closest to the ceiling, your *thickest* string is the low string, because it produces the *lowest* pitch. The *thinnest* string, even though it's nearest the floor, is the high string, because it produces the *highest* pitch.

To summarize:
* The thickest string may be referred to as the bottom, lowest, or fourth string.
* The thinnest string may be referred to as the top, highest, or first string.

Now that we're all on the same page with that, let's move on.

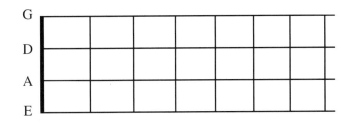

As you can see above, the notes of the four open strings, from lowest pitched to highest pitched, are **E**, **A**, **D**, and **G**. Coincidentally, these are the note names of the four lowest strings (you read the above boxed text, didn't you?) on a guitar, which is one reason why so many bass players double on guitar and vice versa. The fretboard layouts are very similar. (In fact, they're identical when you compare strings 4–1 of the bass with string 6–3 of the guitar. The only difference is that the guitar sounds an octave higher.)

There are all kinds of phrases that people use to remember these notes. Things like **Even Animals Do Gossip** can help in the beginning, but really…it's just four notes. It's not that hard to remember. Coincidentally, the twelfth fret (almost always marked with a special inlay, such as a double dot) of each string is the same note as the open string, only an octave higher. So the twelfth fret of string 4 is E, the twelfth fret of string 3 is A, and so on. Store this information in your mind for later.

SCHOOL IS IN SESSION

The point of the quizzes in this book is to put your new knowledge to the test. If you need to refer back to earlier information, you can do so. But when you actually write the answers down, do so from memory without stopping to look back. The answers to each quiz can be found in the appendix at the end of the book.

I encourage you to actually write and speak the answers instead of just answering in your head. If you don't like the idea of writing in the book, you can write very lightly with a pencil (so it's easily erased), make copies of the quizzes, or just write your answers on a separate piece of paper, making sure to identify the quiz number. The physical act of writing the answers down (and speaking out loud) will aid in your retention of the information.

QUIZ 1
1. Write out the note names of the four open strings.

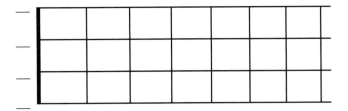

2.

    a) Third open string = ___
    b) First open string = ___
    c) Second open string = ___
    d) Fourth open string = ___

Extra credit:

    a) String 2, fret 12 = ___

    b) String 1, fret 12 = ___

    c) String 4, fret 12 = ___

    d) String 3, fret 12 = ___

NOTES ON THE PIANO

First we'll study a piano keyboard's layout to see how the notes fall. I know, I know. This is supposed to be a bass book, right? Bear with me. The piano is an awesome tool when it comes to learning about notes because of its layout and organization. You don't even need to have a piano or keyboard to make use of this information. The visual is really all you need at this point.

Piano Keyboard Layout

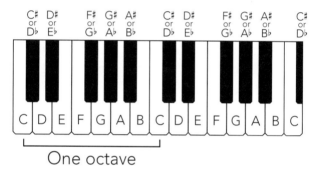

One octave

There are a number of important things to notice here:

- There are white keys and black keys.
- The white-key notes have simple, one-letter names.
- The black keys have names that require additional symbols: The ♯ symbol is a **sharp**. The ♭ symbol is a **flat**. (Sharps and flats are referred to as *accidentals*.)
- When naming a black key to the right of a white key, its name is that white key with a sharp (♯) added to it. In other words, the black key to the right of the white G key is G♯.
- When naming a black key to the left of a white key, its name is that white key with a flat (♭) added to it. In other words, the black key to the left of the white key G is G♭.
- Musical context will determine whether a black key note is named with a sharp or flat; we'll get to that later on.
- The notes progress from left to right up through the alphabet. Once G is reached, we start over again at A. So the musical alphabet consists only of the letters A–G.
- After twelve keys (counting white and black), the pattern begins again in a higher **octave**. A note that's one octave higher than another sounds the same but higher.
- There are two spots where two white keys are right next to each other (with no black keys in between): from B to C and from E to F. This is important, and we'll come back to this point later on.

I don't expect everything in the above list to make sense just yet, but we'll refer back to it several times so it'll be here when you need it. Things will become clearer as we progress. Study the piano key layout until you've memorized the notes, and then try your hand at Quiz 2.

QUIZ 2

1. Identify the grayed keys on the piano keyboard.

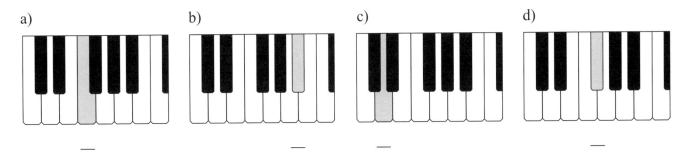

ONE PIANO KEY = ONE FRET

So, we know the piano key layout now. What good does that do? Well, here's the cool thing. **Each key on the piano (including white and black) represents one fret on one string of our bass.** And the notes progress up the string the same way they progress up the keys from left to right on the piano. For example, our open fourth string is an E note. If we look at our piano diagram above, what's the key directly to the right of E? It's an F. The same goes for our bass. The open fourth string is E, and the note on the first fret of the fourth string is F.

THE FOURTH STRING: E

Now let's look at the fourth, or lowest, string and see how it resembles a mini-piano. We've already learned that the open string is E, and the first fret is F. Now let's fill in the rest of the notes up to the twelfth fret.

Fret: 1   2   3   4   5   6   7   8   9   10   11   12

E — F — F♯/G♭ — G — G♯/A♭ — A — A♯/B♭ — B — C — C♯/D♭ — D — D♯/E♭ — E

Look closely back at our first piano key diagram on page 7, and compare the notes from E to E with the fret notes here. You'll see that they appear in the same exact order. So, from the open string to fret 12, the fourth string on our bass is like a mini-piano that spans from E to E an octave higher.

At fret 12, things start all over again. Fret 12 is an E note, which is the same as our open string. So fret 13 is F, fret 14 is F♯/G♭, and so on.

BE CAREFUL WITH THE DOTS!

A typical bass neck will have dot inlays on frets 3, 5, 7, 9, and a double dot on fret 12. (The dots will also continue to appear above fret 12 on frets 15, 17, and 19 usually.) Here's the tricky part. *Most* of these dots on the low E string correspond to "natural" notes—i.e., note names that aren't sharp or flat. Some players fall into the trap of thinking that these dots represent the natural notes, and the frets between mark the accidentals (the sharp or flat notes). But this is not always the case.

Check it out. Fret 3 is a G note, fret 5 is an A note, fret 7 is a B note, but **fret 9 is a C♯ or D♭**. Why is this? Take a look at the piano diagram on page 7 again. Remember how we said there are two spots where two white keys lie right next to each other? One of those spots is between B and C. So, since fret 7 on our fourth string is the note B, then the fret directly above it (fret 8) must be the note C. This means that fret 9 will be C♯/D♭.

You'll find that the dot inlays usually line up with natural notes on all four strings, but they'll be a few spots where this won't be the case, so keep an eye out!

Remember that we said after twelve piano keys (counting white and black keys), the pattern of notes starts over an octave higher. This is confirmed on the bass by the fact that the pattern of notes starts over at fret 12.

QUIZ 3

1. Now that you know this pattern of notes, you can count up the frets, referencing the piano diagram if necessary, and identify any note on the fourth string. (For notes with two names, either one will be acceptable.)

a)

b)

c)

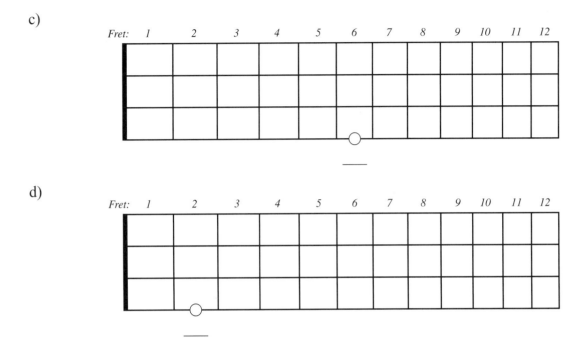

d)

2.

    a) The note on fret 5 is: ___
    b) The note on fret 1 is: ___
    c) The note on fret 11 is: ___
    d) The note between A and B is: ___

Eventually, you won't need to count each fret to find the notes, but the fact that you can do that if necessary is a great start. Many players first become familiar with certain notes and then use them to figure out surrounding ones. For example, the G note at fret 3 on the fourth string is commonly learned early on. Once you know that, it's a simple matter to figure out the surrounding frets: G♭ (or F♯) on fret 2 and G♯ (or A♭) on fret 4.

THE THIRD STRING: A

We'll use the same mini-piano approach to learn the notes on the rest of the strings as well. Since we know the open third string is the note A, we can reference the piano key layout and fill in the fretted notes through to fret 12.

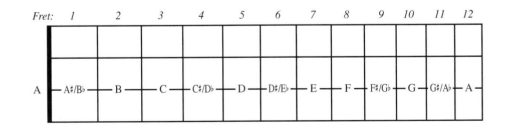

Notice again that the pattern starts over at fret 12. So fret 12 is A, fret 13 is A♯/B♭, fret 14 is B, and so on.

QUIZ 4

1. Identify the notes on the third string, referencing the piano diagram as necessary.

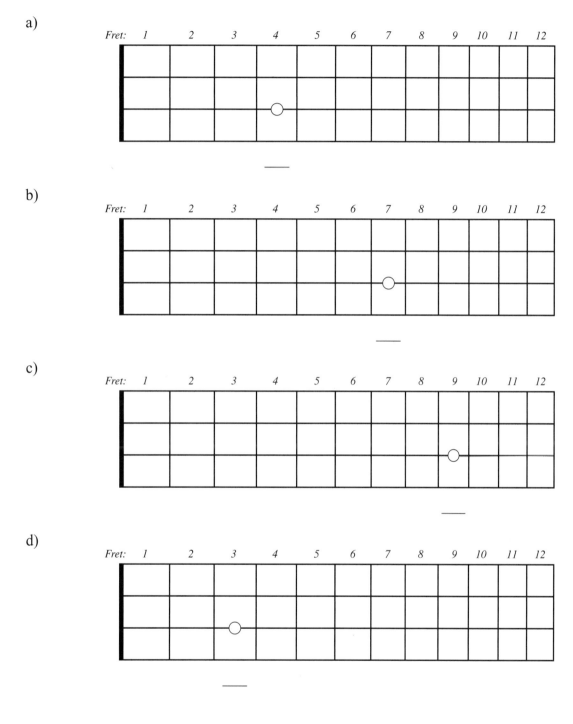

2.

    a) The note on fret 1 is: ___
    b) The note on fret 8 is: ___
    c) The note between F and G is: ___
    d) The note one fret above B is: ___

THE SECOND STRING: D

The fourth string creates a mini-piano from D to D when spanning the open string to fret 12. Let's fill in the rest of the notes.

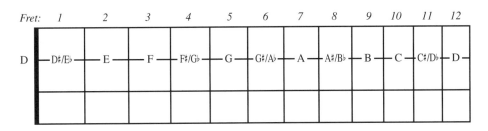

Notice the relationship between the notes on the second string and the ones on the fourth string. The same note on the second string can be found two frets higher than that on the fourth, except we're an octave higher. We'll touch more on this relationship later.

QUIZ 5

1. Identify the notes on the second string, referencing the piano diagram as necessary.

a)

b)

c)

d)

(fretboard diagram: Frets 1–12, open circle at fret 8 with blank below)

2.

    a) The note E♭ is on fret: ___

    b) The note on fret 9 is: ___

    c) The note one fret below G is: ___

    d) The note on fret 2 is: ___

Though not shown, this same pattern of notes starts over again after the twelfth fret. Fret 12 is D, fret 13 is D♯/E♭, fret 14 is E, and so on.

THE FIRST STRING: G

Our mini-piano up to fret 12 on string 1 spans from G to G. Here's how the rest of the notes lay out.

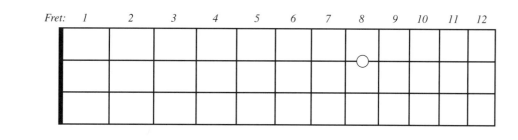

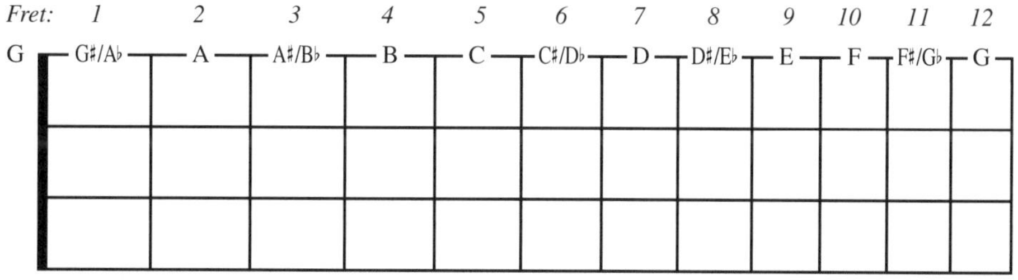

Again, the same two-fret relationship between strings 4 and 2 exists between strings 3 and 1. This type of thing can greatly aid in memorization of the notes, so don't overlook it.

QUIZ 6

1. Identify the notes on the first string, referencing the piano diagram as necessary.

    a)

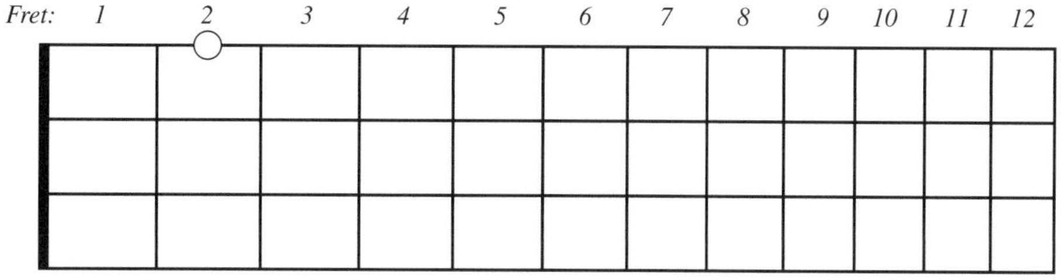

(fretboard diagram: Frets 1–12, open circle at fret 2 with blank below)

b)

Fret:	1	2	3	4	5	6	7	8	9	10	11	12

(marker at fret 6)

_____

c)

Fret:	1	2	3	4	5	6	7	8	9	10	11	12

(marker at fret 10)

_____

d)

Fret:	1	2	3	4	5	6	7	8	9	10	11	12

(marker at fret 8)

_____

2.

   a) The note A♯ is on fret: ___
   b) The note on fret 11 is: ___
   c) The note between D and C is: ___
   d) The note one fret above A is: ___

Again, the pattern starts over twelve frets up. Fret 12 is G, fret 13 is G♯/A♭, fret 14 is A, and so on.

SUMMARY

Here are the things we learned in this chapter:
- The musical alphabet contains the letters A–G.
- There are seven natural notes (white piano keys) and five accidental notes (black piano keys) within one octave.
- There are two spots on the piano keyboard where two white keys appear back to back: from B to C and from E to F.
- One key on a piano (counting both white and black) equals one fret on a string of the bass.
- The black keys on the piano can be named two ways: as a sharp (♯) or as a flat (♭).
- The notes of the open strings on the bass are, from low to high, E–A–D–G.
- The twelfth fret of a string is the same note as the open string, only one octave higher.
- You should know (or at least know how to determine) the notes on each string of the bass.

This is a good start, but we still have a long way to go. Take a breather and, when you're ready, head to Chapter 2.

CHAPTER 2:
INTRODUCTION TO INTERVALS

You may have heard the term **interval** in regards to music before. If you're at all uncertain as to what it means, it's time to get things cleared up once and for all. Intervals are everywhere in music—in every chord, in every melody, in every riff. They're kind of like the Force in Star Wars; they bind the musical universe together and give the musician his/her power. Ok, so maybe that's not an entirely accurate analogy, but it's true that they are everywhere in music!

TWO HALVES MAKE A WHOLE

So what's an interval? Basically, an interval can be described as the *(musical) distance between two notes*. Intervals can be measured as harmonic (when two notes are sounding simultaneously) or melodic (when two notes are sounded one after the other). Since we usually play one note at a time on the bass, we'll deal mostly with melodic intervals. (We'll be working one string at a time in this chapter, so melodic intervals are actually the only possibility.)

We're going to start here with two intervals specifically, both of which are tremendously useful in the music world: the **whole step** and the **half step**. On the bass, a whole step represents the distance of two frets on the same string. So, for example, the interval (distance) from fret 3 to fret 5 on any string is a whole step.

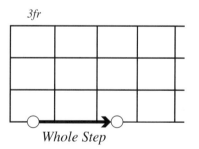
Whole Step

Coincidentally, since we know that the note on fret 3 of string 4 is G and the one on fret 5 is A, we can also say that the interval between the notes G and A is a whole step. Another way you might hear this said is that G and A are a whole step apart from one another.

A half step, as you may by now suspect, is half that of a whole step. In other words, it's the distance of one fret on the same string. The interval from fret 3 to fret 4 on the fourth string, for example, is a half step.

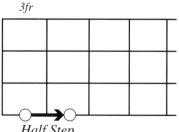
Half Step

Since we know that the note on fret 4 is G♯ or A♭, we can also say that the interval from G to G♯/A♭ is a half step.

To relate this back to our piano keyboard:
- A half step is the distance of one key to the very next (including white and black)
- A whole step is the distance of two keys (including white and black)

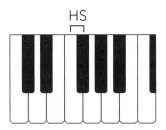

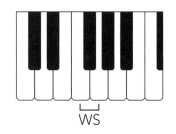

NATURALLY OCCURRING HALF STEPS

Backtracking slightly, if we look back again at the original, two-octave piano key diagram on page 7, remember that we said there were two spots where two white keys lie next to each other: from B to C and from E to F. These are naturally occurring half steps in the musical alphabet. It's as if there's no such thing as a B♯, C♭, E♯, or F♭.

As we'll learn later on, this is not necessarily true, and there will be exceptions when those note names will be used. This, however, doesn't change the fact that there is no note between B and C or E and F. A C note may sometimes be *called* B♯, a B may sometimes be called C♭, an F may sometimes be called E♯, or an E may sometimes be *called* F♭, but that's only a theoretical construct we've applied to help certain musical situations make sense. F♭ will still sound like E, B♯ will sound like C, etc.

These two intervals—whole steps and half steps—have another name as well, which we'll learn in a later chapter. For now, test your mastery of them before we move on.

QUIZ 7

1. Fill in the note names on the neck and identify each interval as either whole step or half step. (For notes with two names, either one will be acceptable.)

a)

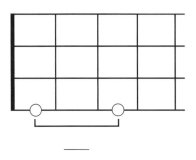

b)

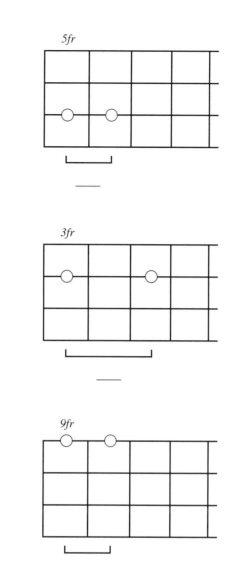

5fr

c)

3fr

d)

9fr

2.
   a) The interval from E to F is a: ____
   b) The interval from G to A♭ is a: ___
   c) The note a whole step above B is: ___
   d) The note a half step below A is: ___

SUMMARY
Here are the things we learned in this chapter:
- An **interval** is the musical distance between notes.
- A **whole step** is the distance of two keys on the piano or two frets on one string of the bass—from G to A, for instance.
- A **half step** is the distance of one key on the piano or one fret on one string of the bass—from G to A♭, for instance.
- A half step is half the distance of a whole step.
- There are two naturally occurring half steps: between B and C and from E to F. These are the two spots within an octave on the keyboard where two white keys lie right next to each other.

Now that we're square on what whole and half steps are, it's time to put them to use. We'll do just that in Chapter 3.

CHAPTER 3:
BUILDING A MAJOR SCALE ON ONE STRING

The major scale is the backbone of Western music. The majority of melodies, bass lines, chords, licks, riffs—you name it—are built from it, and if you could only learn one scale, it would be the major scale.

In this chapter, we're going to use our two new intervals—the whole step and half step—to play a major scale on one string. Obviously, it's not all that common to play scales this way, but it's an excellent way to learn how they're constructed. (We'll get to more traditional scale patterns later.)

THE MAJOR SCALE FORMULA

Every scale is built upon a series of intervals from one note to the next. This is referred to as the scale's *intervallic formula* (or sometimes just "formula"). Most scales contain seven different notes and use only a combination of whole and half steps from note to note. (The "eighth" note, if listed as such, is usually the starting note again only an octave higher.) The starting note of a scale is referred to as the *tonic*, or sometimes the *root*. For example, the tonic of a C major scale is C.

The intervallic formula for every major scale is always the same, and it goes like this:

whole step – whole step – half step – whole step – whole step – whole step – half step

This pattern is often rattled off quickly as "whole whole half, whole whole whole half." Once you know this, you can build a major scale from any tonic you desire.

THE C MAJOR SCALE

For starters, let's create a C major scale. We'll begin with the C note on string 3 at fret 3. Remaining on string 3 throughout, we'll work our way up following the intervals listed in the formula. The first interval listed is a whole step. So we move up a whole step, or two frets, to find the second note: D.

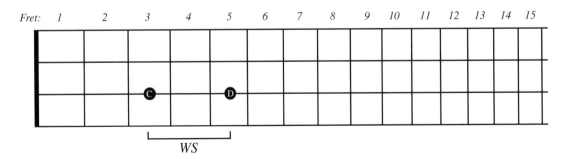

Next is another whole step, so we move up another two frets to the note E.

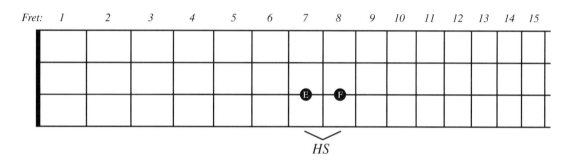

Next is a half step, so we move up one fret to F.

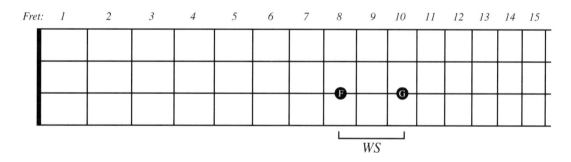

Now another whole step, so we move two frets up to G.

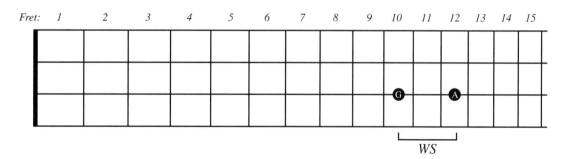

Another whole step takes us up two more frets to A.

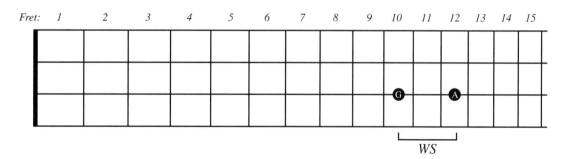

Yet one more whole step takes us up to B.

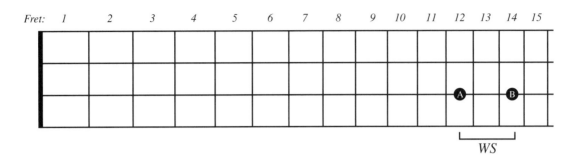

And finally, a half step takes us up to the tonic again, C, an octave higher than where we started.

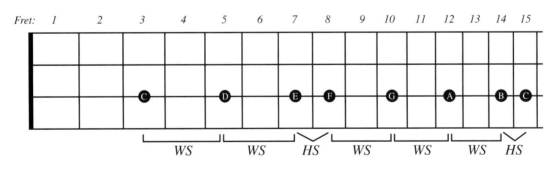

So, again, even though we've listed eight notes here—C, D, E, F, G, A, B, and C—there are actually only seven *different* notes. (There are actually certain types of scales that do have eight or more different notes in them, but the major scale is not one of them.)

So that's all there is to it. We've created the C major scale on one string.

C Major Scale on One String

If you noticed, this scale consists of all natural notes; i.e., there are no sharps or flats. This is the only major scale that can make such a claim. Compare these notes to those on the piano keyboard, and you'll see that they all lie on white keys. Any other major scale will require at least one or more sharps or flats—either sharps or flats, but not both.

LOOK MA, SAME INTERVALS!

To play a different major scale, all we have to do is begin on a different note and follow the same intervallic formula. For example, let's say we begin with the open third string A note. If we follow the whole whole half, whole whole whole half pattern, we'll end up with an A major scale.

A Major Scale on One String

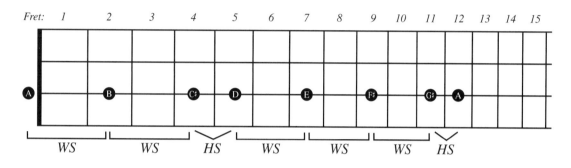

Notice that, in this A major scale, we had to use three accidentals: C♯, F♯, and G♯. This is because we have to stick to the whole whole half, whole whole whole half pattern in order for it to be a major scale. The first whole step move from A to B was fine, but we're supposed to have another whole step after that. However, from B to C is only a half step, so we had to raise C a half step (one fret) up to C♯. The same holds true for the F♯ and G♯ notes.

Let's try one more major scale. We'll build it from F on fret 1 of string 4.

F Major Scale on One String

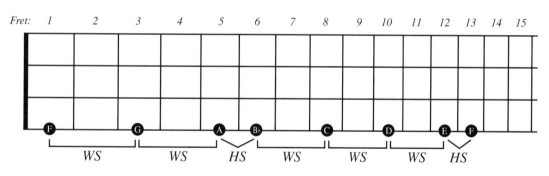

In this scale, we had to make the B note a B♭ note. This is because we need a half step between the third and fourth notes of the scale, and from A to B would be a whole step. So we lower the B note down a half step (one fret) to B♭, and the intervallic formula is perfect.

IS EVERYONE ACCOUNTED FOR? THE ENHARMONIC DILEMMA

As you know, "accidental" notes (i.e., the black keys on the piano) can be called two different names: a sharp note or a flat note. The term for the same note having two different names is *enharmonic*. For example, we would say that G♯ and A♭ are enharmonic to each other. (Actually, any note can be called two different names; it's just that the black keys are the most obvious. Remember earlier we learned that there may be instances where you would call B a C♭, for instance. In that case, B and C♭ are enharmonic.)

So, when building major scales, how do we know which note name to use? Well, it's actually very simple. A major scale has seven different notes (again, the eighth is the same as the first, only an octave higher), so we need seven different note *names* in the scale. This means we need at least one version (natural, sharp, or flat) of every note in the musical alphabet (A–B–C–D–E–F–G) represented when we "spell" a scale.

In our F major scale, for example, we could call the note on fret 6 A♯, but we don't because that would leave us with two versions of an A note (A and A♯) and no version of a B note. Calling the note B♭ results in every note name being used: F–G–A–B♭–C–D–E.

A good habit to get into when figuring out major scales is to start out by writing the letters of the musical alphabet starting on your tonic. Then make the necessary adjustments (flats or sharps). This way, you'll for sure have every note accounted for. For instance, if you want to create a D major scale, start out by writing the seven letters starting from D (plus a high D at the top):

D – E – F – G – A – B – C – D

Then work through the intervallic formula (whole whole half, whole whole whole half), referencing the piano diagram if necessary, and make the necessary adjustments to the notes. You should come up with this:

D–E–F♯–G–A–B–C♯–D

ONE OR THE OTHER – SHARP KEYS AND FLAT KEYS

Since there are twelve notes in an octave (counting white and black keys), then it stands to reason that there are twelve different major scales. These are grouped into sharp keys and flat keys. A major scale in a sharp key is always spelled with sharps only and no flats, and vice versa. So if you're spelling a major scale in a sharp key, and you find yourself with some kind of flat note, you'll know you've made a mistake. Here is how the keys lay out:

C Major (contains no sharps or flats)

Sharp Keys:
G Major (one sharp)
D Major (two sharps)
A Major (three sharps)
E Major (four sharps)
B Major (five sharps)

Flat Keys:
F Major (one flat)
B♭ Major (two flats)
E♭ Major (three flats)
A♭ Major (four flats)
D♭ Major (five flats)

That's eleven keys. The twelfth key is a bit tricky and will appear as either F♯ Major (six sharps) or G♭ Major (six flats). They're the same scale spelled enharmonically.

Later on in the book, we'll learn how these keys are organized in a fashion that makes them fairly easy to memorize. For now, as long as you know the intervallic formula for the major scale, you should be able to work through any key and create its major scale.

QUIZ 8

1. Fill in the missing notes of the following major scales. This will require the most amount of thinking so far! Reference the piano keyboard when you need to. Remember that the major scale formula (W W H, W W W H) must be maintained!

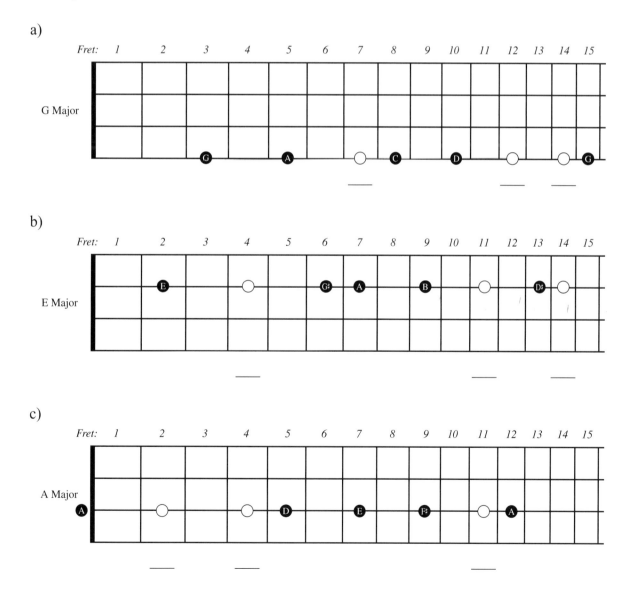

d)

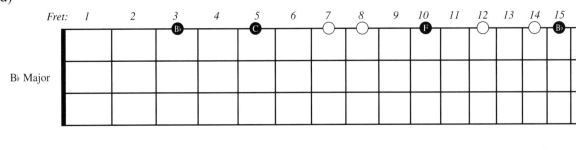

B♭ Major

2.

    a) Spell an E major scale:

    b) Spell an E♭ major scale:

    c) How many flats are in a B♭ major scale and what are they?

    d) How many sharps are in a D major scale and what are they?

SUMMARY

Here are the things we learned in this chapter:

- A major scale contains seven different notes.
- The **intervallic formula** for a major scale: whole–whole–half–whole–whole–whole–half.
- The starting note of a major scale is referred to as the **tonic** or **root**.
- Two notes that sound the same but are spelled differently are **enharmonic**.
- There are sharp keys and flat keys. A major scale will only be built with one or the other. The only major scale that contains neither is C major.
- A major scale must be spelled with seven different letter names.

CHAPTER 4:
MORE WORK WITH INTERVALS

Our interval talk thus far has been limited to whole steps and half steps. Though these two intervals are terribly important, they're really only the tip of the iceberg that is the world of intervals. Now we're going to take a more extensive look at intervals and how they work. This will most likely be the most difficult chapter in the book, so you may want to grab a drink or a snack before you dig in.

NUMBERS AND MORE NUMBERS

Earlier, we dealt briefly with numbers in regards to notes—seven letters in the musical alphabet (A–G), seven white keys, five black keys, etc. Now we'll take this number/note concept a bit further and apply it to intervals. A musical interval has two parts: a **quantity** and a **quality**. The quantity is expressed with a number, while the quality further defines it as a certain type. We'll look at the quantity part now and examine the quality a bit later.

Interval Quantity

The quantity of an interval is a fairly simple concept. You don't even really need an instrument in front of you. It basically just involves counting note names. For example, if we want to know the interval between a C and an E note, we simply count up through the letters of the musical alphabet starting from C:

C (1) – D (2) – E (3)

There are three note names involved, so the distance from C to E is a type of 3rd. That's almost all there is to an interval's quantity. (I say almost, because this isn't the *whole* story, but it's all you need to know for now.) It doesn't take too long to get the hang of it. Just remember that once you reach G, you start back over at A. You don't even really need to concern yourself with sharps and flats; the letter names are the only thing that matters in an interval's quantity.

For example, let's say you want to find the quantity of an interval between the notes A♭ and E. You can just simply ignore the flat sign on the A; don't even worry about it. Just count up the alphabet from A until you reach E.

A (1) – B (2) – C (3) – D (4) – E (5)

So from A♭ to E is a type of 5th. That's all there is to it. Just remember to count through the alphabet from the first note until you reach the second note. Again, this is only half the story of intervals; the other equally important aspect of an interval is the *quality*, which is what we'll look at after this quiz.

WHAT GOES UP, MUST COME DOWN

Although all the examples I've given here are ascending—i.e., counting *up* to another note—you can also measure intervals in descending fashion. In other words, if I asked, what's a 4th below A? You would simply start at A and count *down* four letters.

A (1) – G (2) – F (3) – E (4)

So, a 4th below A is E.

You could also say that E♭ or E♯ is some type of 4th below A, or that E is some type of 4th below A♭ or A♯, and you would be correct, remembering that we're speaking strictly with regards to the quantity at this point. None of those alterations change the fact that there are still four letter names involved.

Let's say you're given two notes and asked to find the interval from the first down to the second—down from A down to F, for example. You can either count down from the first note (A) or up from the second note (F). Either way, you'll come up with the same answer:

Counting down from A: A (1) – G (2) – F (3)

Counting up from F: F (1) – G (2) – A (3)

Either way you count it—down from A or up from F—the distance is a 3rd. Now, if you were to count the opposite ways—*up* from A or *down* from F—you would get a different interval. We'll talk more about that idea later on.

Ok, let's put your knowledge of interval quantities to the test.

QUIZ 9

1. Determine the quantity of the following intervals.
    a) From B up to C: ___
    b) From G up to C: ___
    c) From C down to G: ___
    d) From E down to C: ___

2. Fill in the missing note.
    a) A 4th above the note G is: ___
    b) A 3rd above the note B is: ___
    c) A 7th below the note A is: ___
    d) A 6th below the note C is: ___

Interval Quality

The quality of an interval is the trickier part of the two. Whereas the quantity may tell you an interval is a 3rd, the quality will tell you what *type* of 3rd it is. To learn these, we're going to measure them from the note C (we could pick any note, but starting with C makes things a bit easier in the beginning). We'll compare C with all twelve notes within the range of one octave and examine the name of each interval created. You might want to dog-ear this page, because you'll probably need to refer back to it a few times.

While reading through this chart, play each interval on the third string.

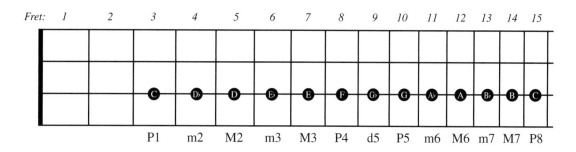

Notes	Number of Half Steps	Name of Interval (quantity and quality)	Abbreviation
C to C	0	perfect unison	P1
C to Db	1	minor 2nd	m2
C to D	2	major 2nd	M2
C to Eb	3	minor 3rd	m3
C to E	4	major 3rd	M3
C to F	5	perfect 4th	P4
C to Gb	6	diminished 5th	d5
C to G	7	perfect 5th	P5
C to Ab	8	minor 6th	m6
C to A	9	major 6th	M6
C to Bb	10	minor 7th	m7
C to B	11	major 7th	M7
C to C	12	perfect octave	P8

I don't expect this to make complete sense to you at this point. Although you should have a good grasp on the quantity (number) aspect, the qualities are probably a bit of a head-scratcher. That will clear up soon if you stick with me!

Let's look at a few of the apparent truths we can deduce from the above table:
- The qualities of major and minor (M, m) apply to 2nds, 3rds, 6ths, and 7ths.
- The quality of perfect (P) applies to unisons, 4ths, 5ths, and octaves.
- A minor interval is one half step smaller than its companion major interval. In other words, C to D is a M2, but C to Db is a m2; C to E is a major 3rd, but C to Eb is m3, etc.
- A diminished interval is one half step smaller than its companion perfect interval. In other words, C to G is a P5, but C to Gb is a d5.

If you were paying attention, you may have noticed that we already have names for two of these intervals. A minor 2nd (m2) is the same thing as a half step, and a major 2nd (M2) is the same thing as a whole step (two half steps make one whole step).

Actually, whole steps are often combined with half steps when measuring intervals. For example, instead of saying a major 3rd is four half steps, you could say it's two whole steps. Instead of saying a perfect 4th is 5 half steps, you could also say it's two and a half steps, etc.

So far, so good? Ok, well, that's not *entirely* all there is to it. Remember when we talked about enharmonic notes? This is the term for two notes that sound the same but have different names, such as F♯ and G♭ or C♯ and D♭. Well, intervals can be enharmonic as well. What happens if we look at the same chart but we substitute enharmonic notes when possible? In other words, we'll be using the sharp names for notes instead of the flat ones. Let's check it out.

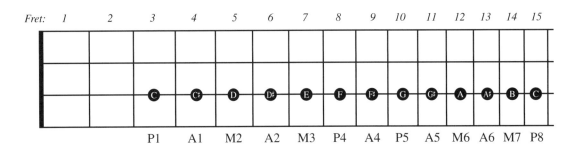

Notes	Number of Half Steps	Name of Interval (quantity and quality)	Abbreviation
C to C	0	perfect unison	P1
C to C♯	1	augmented unison	A1
C to D	2	major 2nd	M2
C to D♯	3	augmented 2nd	A2
C to E	4	major 3rd	M3
C to F	5	perfect 4th	P4
C to F♯	6	augmented 4th	A4
C to G	7	perfect 5th	P5
C to G♯	8	augmented 5th	A5
C to A	9	major 6th	M6
C to A♯	10	augmented 6th	A6
C to B	11	major 7th	M7
C to C	12	perfect octave	P8

Pretty crazy, huh? All of a sudden, all of these "augmented" intervals pop up. From this chart, we can add to our deductions above with this apparent truth:

- An augmented interval is one half step larger than its companion perfect or major interval. In other words, C to D is a M2, but C to D♯ is an A2; C to F is a P4, but C to F♯ is an A4.

Let's examine these oddball names a bit more closely:

- **Augmented unison (C to C♯)**: This is really kind of an oddball, and more of a theoretical construct than anything. According to our law of quantity, since only one letter name is used here, we can't call it a minor 2nd. It has to be some kind of unison. So, since a normal unison (C to C) is called a "perfect" unison, which is in itself kind of funny, we have to treat C to C♯ as an augmented unison.
- **Augmented 2nd (C to D♯)**: This interval, as with the remaining ones, is one that you will occasionally see in actual practice. It's the same amount of half steps (three) as a m3, but since only two letter names are used, we can't call it a 3rd.
- **Augmented 4th (C to F♯)**: This interval is actually used just as often as its enharmonic equivalent— the diminished 5th (C to G♭). At six half steps, it marks the half way point of the octave. It sounds evil, and it's also known as the "tritone" (because it's the distance of three whole steps). This interval was avoided in earlier centuries because people feared it was the work of the devil.
- **Augmented 5th (C to G♯)**: This is another one you'll see fairly often in music, though its enharmonic equivalent, the minor 6th, is certainly more common.
- **Augmented 6th (C to A♯)**: You will run into this interval once in a blue moon, especially if you study classical music, but its enharmonic name, the minor 7th, is much, much more common.

The specific musical situation will determine what we call a certain interval. (Just as, for instance, the reason we call the fourth note of an F major scale a B♭ instead of A♯ is because we need each letter name represented in the scale.) As mentioned, there are times when the above, less-common names are used (with the exception of the tritone, which is commonly referred to as an A4 or a d5), but most musical situations will require the use of the names shown in the first chart. (Believe it or not, there will be times when you'll call an interval by a name not shown on either of these charts, but we don't need to worry about that yet at all.)

Ready to test yourself on these? Study the previous two charts until you've got a handle on them, and then step up to bat.

QUIZ 10

1. Determine the full name (quality and quantity) of the following intervals. If you get lost, remember: first count the letter names to determine the proper quantity, then count the half steps to determine the quality. We'll only deal with ascending intervals in this quiz, as descending ones can be a bit tricky at this point.

    a) From B up to C: ____
    b) From G up to C: ____
    c) From C up to G♯: ____
    d) From E up to C: ____

2. Fill in the missing note.

    a) A perfect 4th above the note F is: ____
    b) A minor 3rd above the note B is: ____
    c) A major 7th above the note A is: ____
    d) An augmented 4th above the note C is: ____

SUMMARY

Here are the things we learned in this chapter:

- Intervals consist of two parts: a **quantity** and a **quality**.
- The quantity of an interval is determined solely by counting the letter names involved; the quality is then determined by the number of half steps (or whole steps) present between the two notes.
- There are five types of qualities we may assign to an interval: **major**, **minor**, **augmented**, **diminished**, and **perfect**.
- Major and minor qualities are commonly used for 2nds, 3rds, 6ths, and 7ths.
- Perfect, augmented, and diminished intervals are commonly used for unisons, 4ths, 5ths, and octaves.
- A minor interval is one half step smaller than a major one; i.e., a m2 is one half step, and a M2 is two half steps (or one whole step).
- A diminished interval is one half step smaller, and an augmented interval is one half step greater, than a perfect one. A P5 is seven half steps; a d5 is 6 half steps, and an A5 is 8 half steps.
- The interval of a d5 or its enharmonic equivalent, the A4, is known as a **tritone**.

Ok, you can pick up your bass again, because now we're going to start applying some of this knowledge to the fretboard once more.

CHAPTER 5:
MAJOR SCALE PATTERNS

It's time to learn how to express these intervals on the fretboard. We've learned a great deal of information about how they work, so now let's see how they're played. You already know how to play the intervals on one string, so now let's stop traversing the length of the neck and learn how to finger these things while remaining in one position (as much as possible). This will also allow us, for the first time, to play these as harmonic as well as melodic intervals.

INTERVALS OF THE MAJOR SCALE

A great way to get started is by reexamining the major scale. We already learned the formula "whole whole half, whole whole whole half." Now we're going to measure all the intervals from the tonic of the scale. In doing so, we'll not only learn commonly used fingerings for the major scale, but we'll also learn commonly used fingerings for many intervals as well.

Let's work with the C major scale here to start with. As you know, the notes of the C major scale are C–D–E–F–G–A–B–C. Let's compare each note back to the tonic C and measure its interval.

C to D: M2 (two half steps)

The second note in the scale (D) is a major 2nd above the tonic C. Since this is such a small distance, we'll finger it on the same (third) string.

Major 2nd

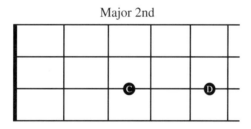

C to E: M3 (four half steps)

The third note (E) is a major 3rd above the tonic. Fingering this note on the third string would take us higher up the neck than we'd like to go, so we're going to move the note to the second string.

Major 3rd

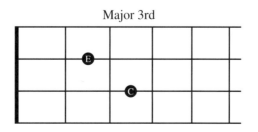

C to F: P4 (five half steps)

The fourth note (F) is a perfect 4th above the tonic. Since it's only a half step above the third note, we'll stay on string 2.

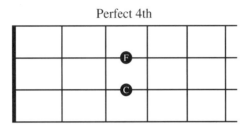

Perfect 4th

C to G: P5 (seven half steps)

The fifth note (G) is a perfect 5th above the tonic. We can finger it on string 2 as well without moving our hand position.

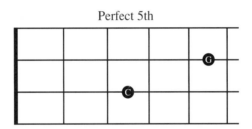

Perfect 5th

C to A: M6 (nine half steps)

The sixth note (A) is a major 6th above the tonic. In order to stay in our current position, we'll move it to the first string.

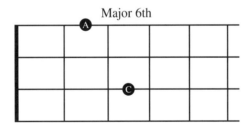

Major 6th

C to B: M7 (eleven half steps)

The seventh note (B) is a major 7th above the tonic.

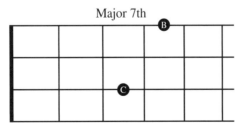

Major 7th

C to C: P8 (twelve half steps)

And finally, the eighth note is an octave above the tonic—i.e., the same note name.

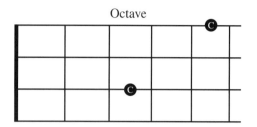
Octave

Notice that we only have two different qualities in the major scale when measuring each note against the tonic: major and perfect.

So, let's check out the major scale pattern we created. This is a C major scale in second position (because the first finger of the fretting hand is positioned at the second fret). The tonic notes are indicated with open circles.

C Major Scale

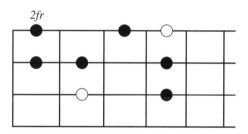
2fr

MOVEABLE SCALE FORMS

The above is a **moveable scale form** because it contains no open strings. This means that we can slide the whole form up or down the neck to play a major scale from different tonics. For example, if we played this scale form up a whole step (two frets) in fourth position, we'd have a D major scale.

D MAJOR SCALE

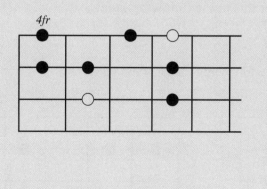
4fr

We can also move this whole scale form down a string set, so that the low tonic note begins on the fourth string. This is because the bass is tuned in perfect 4th intervals, so the intervallic pattern of notes on strings 3–1 will be the same as on strings 4–2. For example, we could move our C major scale pattern above down a string set to strings 4–2, and we'd have a G major scale, because the tonic note would be G.

G MAJOR SCALE

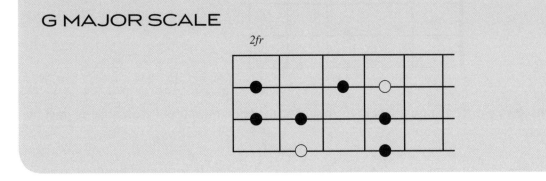

Interval Shapes

In this process, we also learned fingerings for seven different intervals. Since no open strings were used, all of these interval fingerings are moveable as well. Let's review the interval shapes. (We'll eventually learn how to finger the M2 interval on adjacent strings.)

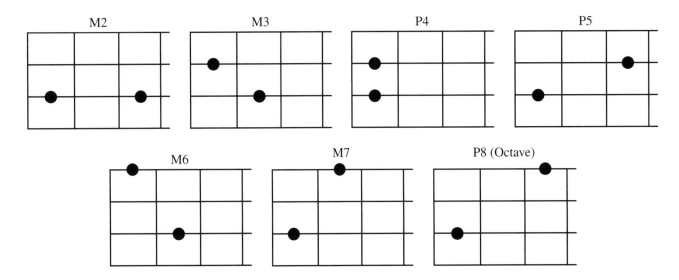

Just as with the major scale form, you can also move these interval shapes down a string set. And for the shapes on the same or adjacent strings, which include the M2, M3, P4, and P5, you can also move up a string set as well. Watch out for this in the following quiz!

QUIZ 11

1. Fill in the missing dots in the following major scale patterns.

a)   b)

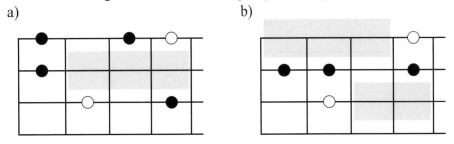

2. Write out the following major scales on the blank grids, providing the appropriate fret numbers if necessary. Use moveable forms only (no open strings). (Since you can base the form off the third or fourth string, there will be two possible correct answers for each scale; either one will be acceptable.)

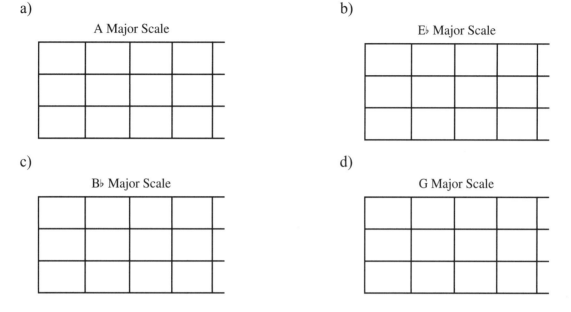

a)

A Major Scale

b)

E♭ Major Scale

c)

B♭ Major Scale

d)

G Major Scale

3. Identify the following intervals.

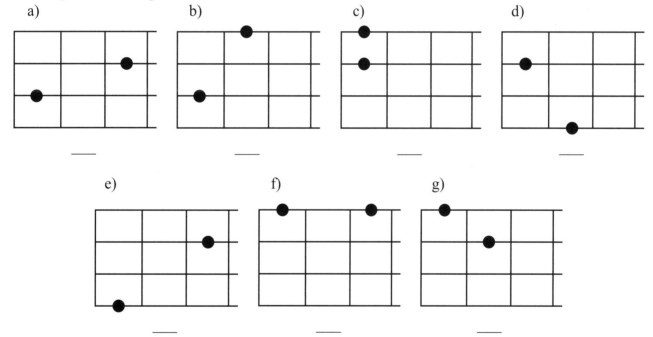

a)

b)

c)

d)

e)

f)

g)

SUMMARY

Here are the things we learned in this chapter:

- When measuring the interval between the tonic and every other note of the major scale, we get the following intervals: M2, M3, P4, P5, M6, M7, and P8.
- A **moveable shape** is one in which there are no open strings.
- We learned a moveable major scale pattern that can be played with its root (or tonic) anywhere along the third or fourth string to create different major scales.
- We learned moveable interval shapes for the above listed intervals.

CHAPTER 6:
THE MINOR SCALE

All of our work with scales thus far has dealt with the major scale. It's by far the most commonly used scale in Western music, but there are many others in use as well. In this chapter we'll look at the major scale's gothic sibling: the **minor scale**.

A DIFFERENT TYPE OF SCALE FORMULA

In order to learn the minor scale, we're going to take a quick detour. We've already learned one formula with regards to scale construction: the intervallic formula. For a major scale, this is the WWH, WWWH formula we've seen so often. But scales are also known by a *numeric formula*. We'll use this method for learning the minor scale.

The major scale is the standard by which we judge all other scales when it comes to the numeric formula. To create the numeric formula for a major scale, we simply assign a number to each note: 1 through 7. So we would say that a major scale's numeric formula is:

$$1 - 2 - 3 - 4 - 5 - 6 - 7$$

By itself, this doesn't seem to be of any use. But it's extremely useful when we want to build another type of scale, such as the minor scale. The minor scale (or natural minor scale) is another extremely common scale that's used in all styles of music; its numeric formula is:

$$1 - 2 - \flat3 - 4 - 5 - \flat6 - \flat7$$

So what does this mean? Well, it simply means that, in order to turn a major scale (with its formula of 1–2–3–4–5–6–7) into a minor scale, we need to flat (lower by one half step) the third, sixth, and seventh notes. Let's look at C major as an example.

C major scale: C–D–E–F–G–A–B
C minor scale: C–D–E♭–F–G–A♭–B♭

A minor scale also has an intervallic formula of whole and half steps:

whole – half – whole – whole – half – whole – whole

Let's take a look at a C minor scale played entirely on the third string.

C Minor Scale on One String

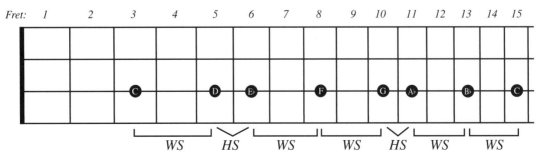

Compare this to the original C major scale diagram on page 20, and you'll see that the only differences are:

- the 3rd (E) has been lowered a half step to E♭
- the 6th (A) has been lowered a half step to A♭
- the 7th (B) has been lowered a half step to B♭

INTERVALS OF THE MINOR SCALE

Now we're going to measure all the intervals from the tonic of the scale. In doing so, we'll not only learn commonly used fingerings for the minor scale, but we'll also learn commonly used fingerings for many intervals as well.

Let's continue working with the C minor scale. As you now know, the notes of the C minor scale are C–D–E♭–F–G–A♭–B♭–C. Let's compare each note back to the tonic C and measure its interval.

C to D: M2 (two half steps)

The second note in the scale (D) is a major 2nd above the tonic C. Since this is such a small distance, we'll finger it on the same (third) string.

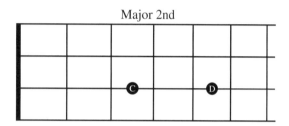

Major 2nd

C to E♭: m3 (three half steps)

The third note (E♭) is a minor 3rd above the tonic. Fingering this note on the second string would require a good stretch between the 2nd and ♭3rd, so we're going to keep it on the third string.

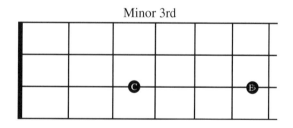

Minor 3rd

C to F: P4 (five half steps)

The fourth note (F) is a perfect 4th above the tonic. We'll move to string 2 for this note.

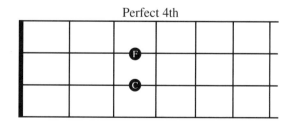

Perfect 4th

C to G: P5 (seven half steps)

The fifth note (G) is a perfect 5th above the tonic. We can finger it on string 2 as well without moving our hand position.

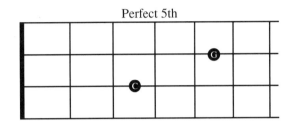

Perfect 5th

C to A♭: m6 (eight half steps)

The sixth note (A♭) is a minor 6th above the tonic. Since this is just a half step above the 5th, we'll remain on string 2.

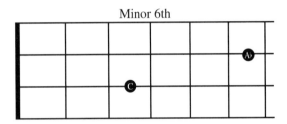

Minor 6th

C to B♭: m7 (ten half steps)

The seventh note (B♭) is a minor 7th above the tonic. We'll move to string 1 for this note.

Minor 7th

C to C: P8 (twelve half steps)

And finally, the eighth note is an octave above the tonic—i.e., the same note name.

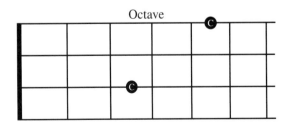

Octave

Notice that, whereas we only had two different qualities in the major scale when measuring each note against the tonic (major and perfect), the minor scale adds the minor quality as well. Also be sure to see that only the notes we changed—i.e., the 3rd, 6th, and 7th—had different interval names.

So, let's check out the minor scale pattern we created. This is a C minor scale in third position (because the first finger of the fretting hand is positioned at the third fret). The tonic notes are indicated with open circles.

C Minor Scale

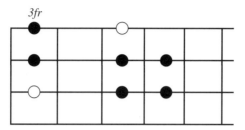

Again, this is a moveable scale form, so we can move up a whole up step (two frets) to play a D minor scale, for example.

D Minor Scale

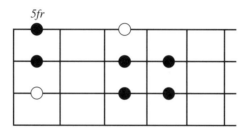

Or, we can move the pattern down a string set and play it on strings 4–2. If we do this and begin in third position, we have a G minor scale.

G Minor Scale

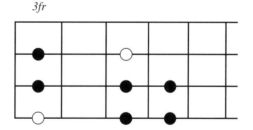

Interval Shapes

In this process, we also learned fingerings for three new intervals. Since no open strings were used, all of these interval fingerings are moveable as well. Let's review the new interval shapes. (We'll eventually learn how to finger the m3 interval on adjacent strings.)

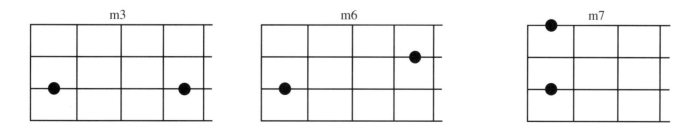

Just as with the major scale form, you can also move these interval shapes down a string set. And for the shapes on the same or adjacent strings, which include the m3 and m6, you can also move up a string set as well. Watch out for this in the following quiz!

QUIZ 12

1. Fill in the missing dots in the following minor scale patterns.

a)   b)

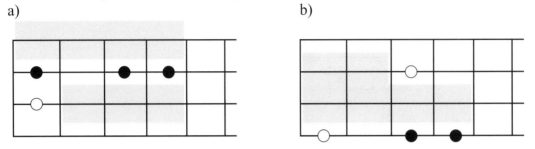

2. Write out the following minor scales on the blank grids, providing the appropriate fret numbers if necessary. Use moveable forms only (no open strings!). (Since you can base the form off the third or fourth string, there will be two possible correct answers for each scale; either one will be acceptable.)

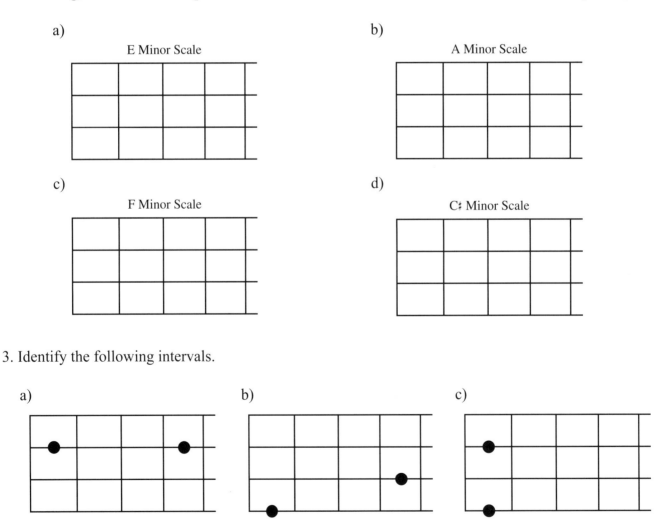

a)

E Minor Scale

b)

A Minor Scale

c)

F Minor Scale

d)

C♯ Minor Scale

3. Identify the following intervals.

a)   b)   c)

_____   _____   _____

d)   e)   f)

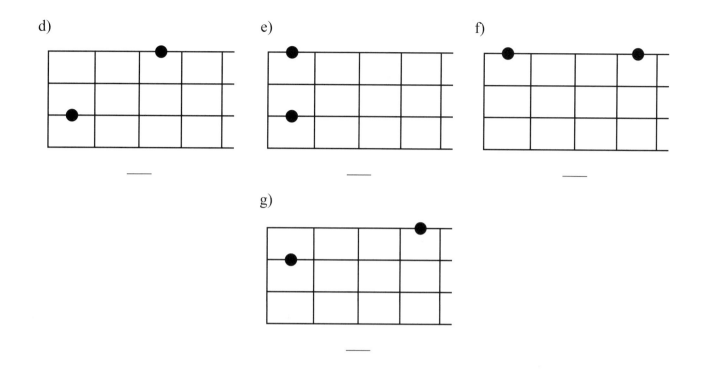

g)

___

SUMMARY

Here are the things we learned in this chapter:

- When measuring the interval between the tonic and every other note of the minor scale, we get the following intervals: M2, m3, P4, P5, m6, m7, and P8.
- The numeric formula for a minor scale is 1–2–♭3–4–5–♭6–♭7.
- The intervallic formula for a minor scale is whole–half–whole–whole–half–whole–whole.
- We learned a moveable minor scale pattern that can be played with its root (or tonic) anywhere along the third or fourth string to create different minor scales.
- We learned moveable interval shapes for the above listed intervals.

CHAPTER 7:
MORE INTERVAL SHAPES AND SCALE PATTERNS

We've learned how to play a great deal of intervals thus far. To review, here's a list of the intervals for which you should know a shape on the fretboard:

M2	m6
m3	M6
M3	m7
P4	M7
P5	P8

This is a good start, and it covers all the notes in the major and minor scales, but there are still several other intervals out there (as we've seen). Now's the time to learn the whole kit and caboodle—every interval within the octave.

If you remember, for two of the intervals listed above, we learned how to play them on one string. From now on, every interval we play with involve two notes played on different strings, so you'll always be able to play them as harmonic or melodic intervals. Let's get to it!

THE CHROMATIC SCALE

When we play every single note within the range of an octave, we're playing what's known as the **chromatic scale**. It's not really necessary to learn a fingering pattern for this "scale," as it's not really something you'll use in that way—with the exception of maybe some finger exercises to warm up or to work on coordination.

You'll also hear the term chromatic used to mean several half steps in a row. For example, you might hear, "Play chromatically from G down to E." This would mean you would play the notes G, G♭ (or F♯), F, and E.

ALL TWELVE INTERVALS WITHIN ONE OCTAVE

Several of these intervals will be shown in two different shapes—one on adjacent strings and the other on non-adjacent strings. So you'll also learn some other options for a few of the shapes you already know. It's highly recommended to become familiar with both options. Note that the more common interval names are listed first and their enharmonic equivalents, when applicable, are listed second.

Unison (P1)

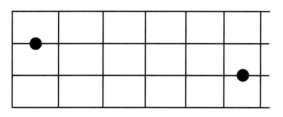

Minor 2nd (m2)

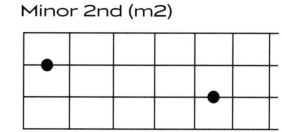

Major 2nd (M2)

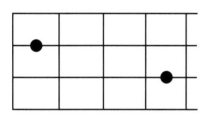

Minor 3rd (m3) or Augmented 2nd (A2)

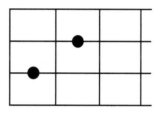

Major 3rd (M3)

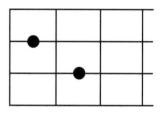

Perfect 4th (P4)

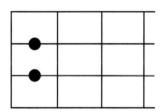

Augmented 4th (A4) or Diminished 5th (d5)

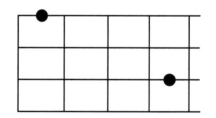

Perfect 5th (P5)

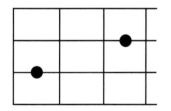

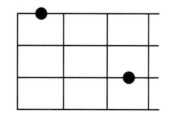

Minor 6th (m6) or Augmented 5th (A5)

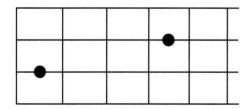

Major 6th (M6)

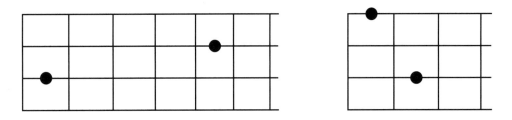

Minor 7th (m7) or Augmented 6th (A6)

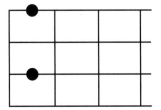

Major 7th (M7)

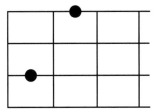

We played these based off a note on the third string, but again, you could move them all down a string set and base them off a note on the fourth string. You could also move the first several up a string set and base them off a note on the second string. The shapes would remain the same, relative to the new string set. Watch out for this in the quiz!

QUIZ 13

1. Identify the following intervals.

a)   b)   c)

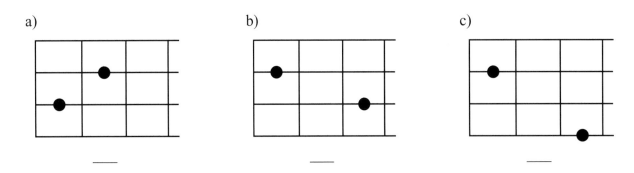

____   ____   ____

d)   e)

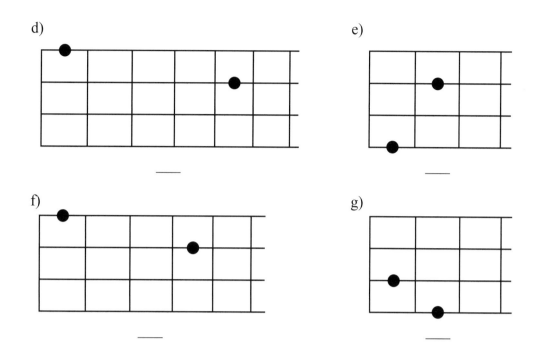

_____   _____

f)   g)

_____   _____

2. Complete the following interval shape by adding the top note.

a)

P4

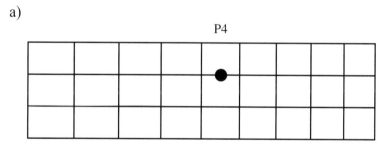

b)

A5

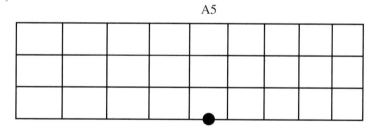

c)

m2

d)

m3

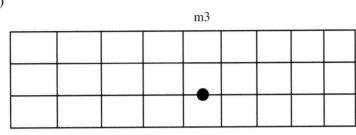

e)

m7

f)

M6

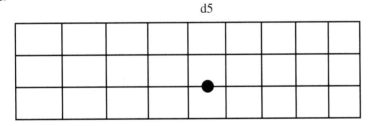

g)

d5

h)

A2

Extra credit:

Now put all of your knowledge of intervals to the test. For each interval, start with the given note and add the interval above it, including the correct note name as well. The first example is completed for you. Watch out for letter H; it's tricky!

a)

Start with: C, Str. 3   Add: M3

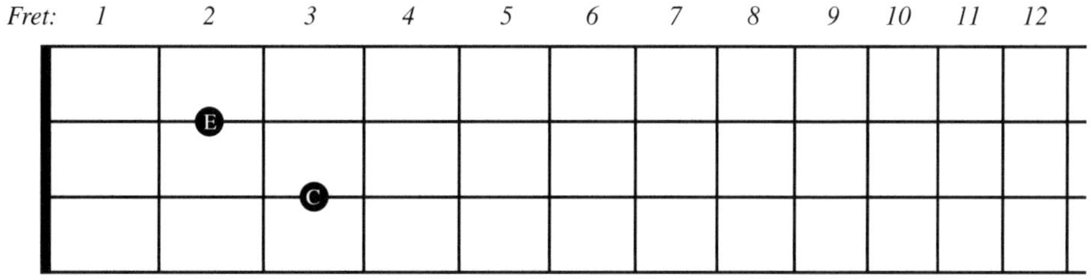

Fret:	*1*	*2*	*3*	*4*	*5*	*6*	*7*	*8*	*9*	*10*	*11*	*12*

b)

Start with: D, Str. 3   Add: m6

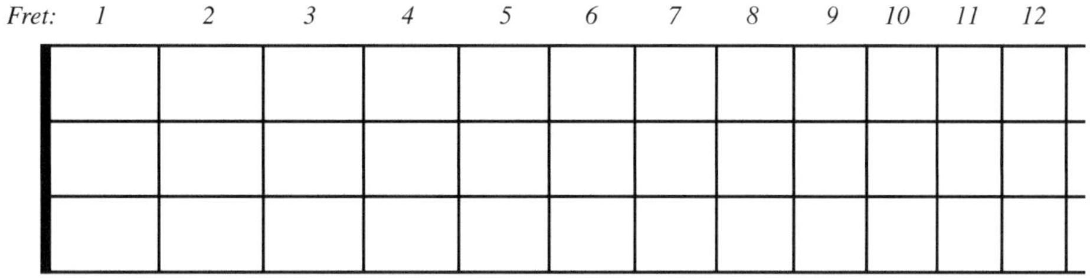

Fret:	*1*	*2*	*3*	*4*	*5*	*6*	*7*	*8*	*9*	*10*	*11*	*12*

c)

Start with: F, Str. 4   Add: m7

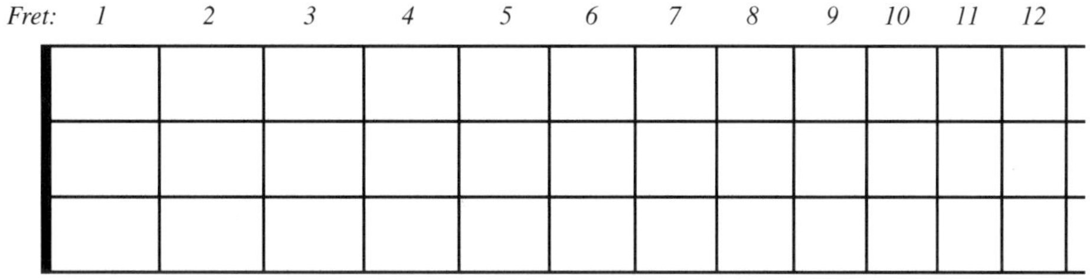

Fret:	*1*	*2*	*3*	*4*	*5*	*6*	*7*	*8*	*9*	*10*	*11*	*12*

d)

Start with: A♭, Str. 4   Add: P5

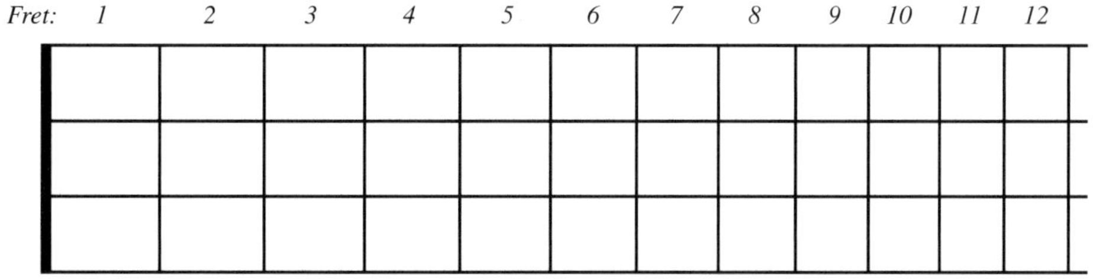

Fret:	*1*	*2*	*3*	*4*	*5*	*6*	*7*	*8*	*9*	*10*	*11*	*12*

e)

Start with: E♭, Str. 3   Add: P4

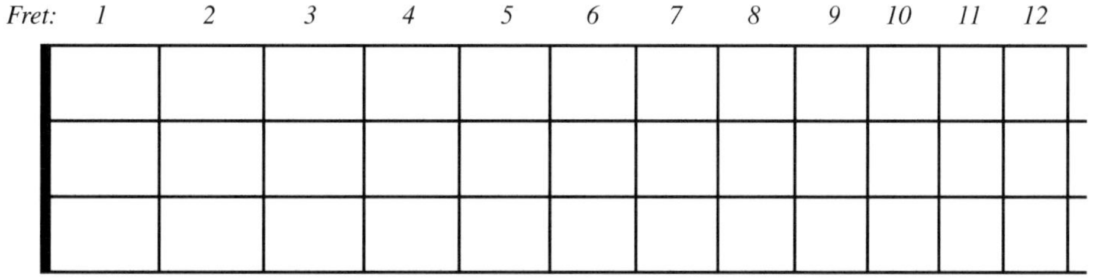

Fret:	*1*	*2*	*3*	*4*	*5*	*6*	*7*	*8*	*9*	*10*	*11*	*12*

f)

Start with: B, Str. 3   Add: M7

Fret: 1   2   3   4   5   6   7   8   9   10   11   12

g)

Start with: C♯, Str. 2   Add: m3

Fret: 1   2   3   4   5   6   7   8   9   10   11   12

h)

Start with: B♭, Str. 2   Add: m2

Fret: 1   2   3   4   5   6   7   8   9   10   11   12

ALTERNATIVE MAJOR AND MINOR SCALE PATTERNS

So far, we've learned one moveable pattern for the major scale and one moveable pattern for the minor scale. Now that we've mastered several more interval shapes, it seems like a good time to expand our scale pattern repertoire. Whereas our previous scale patterns began with either the first (major scale) or second (minor scale) finger, these patterns will begin with the fourth finger.

Alternative Major Scale Pattern – C Major Scale

Here's an alternative moveable major scale pattern. We'll play this one in fifth position, which will make it a C major scale.

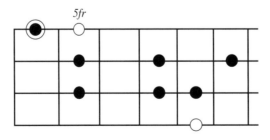

Note that the seventh note (B) can optionally be fingered on string 1 by shifting back to fourth position briefly.

Since this scale pattern uses all four strings, it can not be moved up a string set. Therefore, the low tonic note will always be based off string 4.

Alternative Minor Scale Pattern – C Minor Scale

Now let's take a look at another moveable minor scale pattern. Again, we'll play in fifth position, making this a C minor scale.

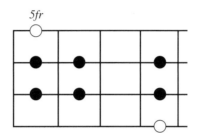

This pattern also uses all four strings, so it too will always be based off a fourth-string low tonic.

QUIZ 14

1. Write out the following major or minor scale shapes using the alternative patterns we just covered. Label the first fret in each diagram to show position when necessary. If the pattern is too low on the neck, take it up an octave (up twelve frets). The first example is done for you.

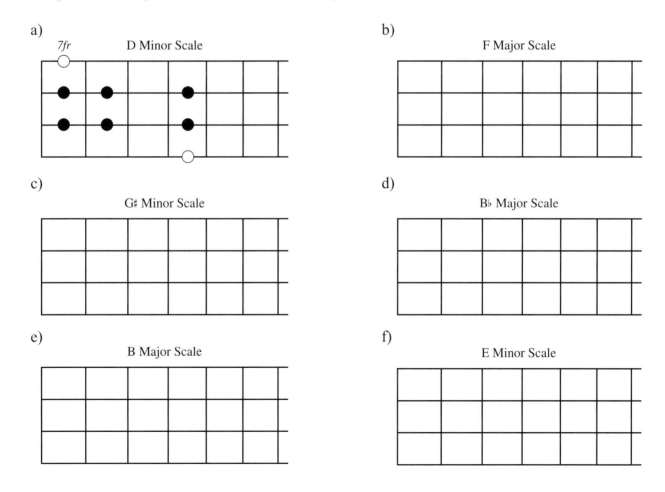

a) D Minor Scale (7fr)

b) F Major Scale

c) G♯ Minor Scale

d) B♭ Major Scale

e) B Major Scale

f) E Minor Scale

g)

D♭ Major Scale

h)

A Minor Scale

SUMMARY

Here are the things we learned in this chapter:

- A **chromatic scale** contains all twelve notes within one octave (all white and black keys on the piano)
- We learned how to play every moveable shape of every chromatic interval within the range of one octave.
- There are two useable fingerings for several of the intervals within the octave range; they can be played on adjacent strings or non-adjacent strings.
- We learned an alternative moveable pattern for the major scale based off the fourth string.
- We learned an alternative moveable pattern for the minor scale also based off the fourth string.

CHAPTER 8:
TRIADS

What's a triad? It's a chord with three different notes (hence the name). Although we don't often play chords on the bass, per se, knowledge of triads and how they're constructed is tremendously helpful when it comes to creating intelligent bass lines. Therefore, it's imperative to get them under our fingers.

YET MORE FORMULAS

Just as scales have intervallic and numeric formulas, so do triads. Numeric formulas are the most useful with regards to triads, so we'll be using those. There are four triads we're going to look at: **major**, **minor**, **augmented**, and **diminished**. As you no doubt recognize, all four of these are also interval qualities.

Just as we altered the numeric formula of the major scale to form the minor scale, we can do the same thing to form different triads.

ARPEGGIOS: FUNNY NAME, SIMPLE CONCEPT

Although it is possible to play triads as chords on the bass, we won't concern ourselves with that. They tend to sound muddy in all but the upper registers of the fretboard, and our reason for studying them isn't to become proficient chord players. We want to understand the notes that comprise them so we'll be better equipped to support them with our bass lines.

Therefore, we'll play the notes of these triads as arpeggios. This simply means that, instead of sounding all the notes of the chord at once (the way pianists and guitarists often do), we'll be playing through them one at a time. This can still suggest the sound of the chord, and it won't muddy things up either.

Of course, many players do occasionally play chords on the bass, and they can sound great in the right circumstances. If this is something that interests you, I encourage you to work out the fingerings and give it a try.

MAJOR TRIAD (1–3–5)

The process used to create triads is sometimes referred to as "stacking 3rds." If we want to build a C major triad, for example, we start by looking at the C major scale: C–D–E–F–G–A–B. To stack 3rds, we begin with the tonic, or 1, move up a 3rd to E, and then move up another 3rd to G. We'll be using every other note of the scale.

C – D – **E** – F – **G** – A – B

These three notes (C, E, and G) form a C major triad. The C in this case is known as the **root** of the chord. (Whereas "tonic" and "root" are sometimes used interchangeably to describe the first note of a scale, the term "tonic" is not often used to describe the first note of a chord.) Since we don't alter any of the notes, we didn't stray from the major scale's numeric formula. So we can say the **formula for a major triad is 1–3–5**, or **root–3rd–5th**. In other words, we just use the first, third, and fifth notes of the root's major scale.

We can also measure each note's interval from the root. If we do this, we'll find that a major triad contains the following:

- **Major 3rd (M3)**: from root to 3rd
- **Perfect 5th (P5)**: from root to 5th

Major Triad – Shape 1

So let's take a look at some moveable shapes for a major triad. This first one is based off our first major scale pattern and uses the second finger on the root, which is indicated with an open circle.

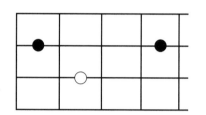

We can also move this exact shape up or down a string set to play an arpeggio from a different root note.

Major Triad – Shape 2

Our second shape is based off our alternative pattern for the major scale and uses the fourth finger on the root.

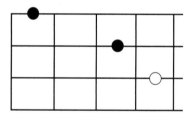

Since this shape uses three adjacent strings, we can't move it up a string set. But we can move it down a string set with the root on the fourth string.

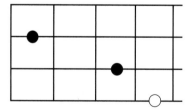

QUIZ 15

1. How many notes are in a triad? _____

2. What is the formula for a major triad? _____

3. Spell the following triads. (Remember, you're just using the first, third, and fifth notes of each root's respective major scale. So you'll need to spell the major scale first, if necessary.)

    a) A major: _____
    b) D major: _____
    c) B♭ major: _____
    d) F major: _____

4. Write diagrams for the following triad arpeggios on the fretboard. Use an open circle to indicate the root, and use a fret marker to indicate position. Be sure to place the root note on the specified string and use the specified shape. The first example is done for you.

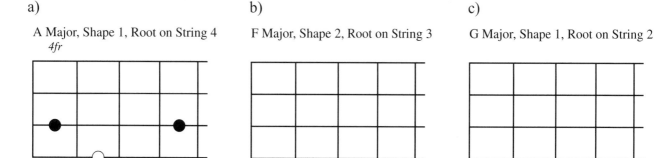

a)

    A Major, Shape 1, Root on String 4
    4fr

b)

    F Major, Shape 2, Root on String 3

c)

    G Major, Shape 1, Root on String 2

d)

    E♭ Major, Shape 2, Root on String 4

e)

    A♭ Major, Shape 1, Root on String 2

f)

    B Major, Shape 1, Root on String 3

MINOR TRIAD (1–♭3–5)

The only difference between a minor triad and the major triad is that the 3rd is lowered a half step. (The same exact thing happens in the minor scale—remember?) So, to form a C minor triad, for example, we start with the C major scale (C–D–E–F–G–A–B), take the first, third, and fifth notes (C–E–G), and then lower the 3rd by a half step.

So a C minor triad would be spelled **C–E♭–G**. Its formula is **1–♭3–5**, or **root, ♭3rd, 5th**. Coincidentally, this is the same thing as using the first, third, and fifth notes of the root's minor scale.

We can also measure each note's interval from the root. If we do this, we'll find that a minor triad contains the following:

- **Minor 3rd (m3)**: from root to ♭3rd
- **Perfect 5th (P5)**: from root to 5th

Minor Triad – Shape 1

This first moveable minor triad shape is based off our first minor scale pattern and uses the first finger on the root, which is indicated with an open circle.

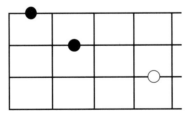

We can also move this exact shape up or down a string set to play an arpeggio from a different root note.

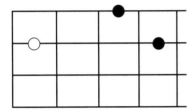
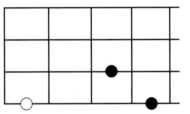

Minor Triad – Shape 2

Our second shape is based off our alternative pattern for the minor scale and uses the fourth finger on the root.

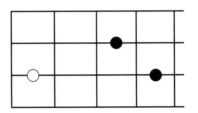

Since this shape uses three adjacent strings, we can't move it up a string set. But we can move it down a string set with the root on the fourth string.

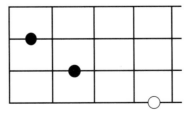

QUIZ 16

1. What is the formula for a minor triad? _____

2. Spell the following triads. (Remember, you're just using the first, third, and fifth notes of each root's respective minor scale. So you'll need to spell the minor scale first, if necessary.)

    a) A minor: _____
    b) D minor: _____
    c) C♯ minor: _____
    d) F♯ minor: _____

3. Write diagrams for the following triad arpeggios on the fretboard. Use an open circle to indicate the root, and use a fret marker to indicate position. Be sure to place the root note on the specified string and use the specified shape. The first example is done for you.

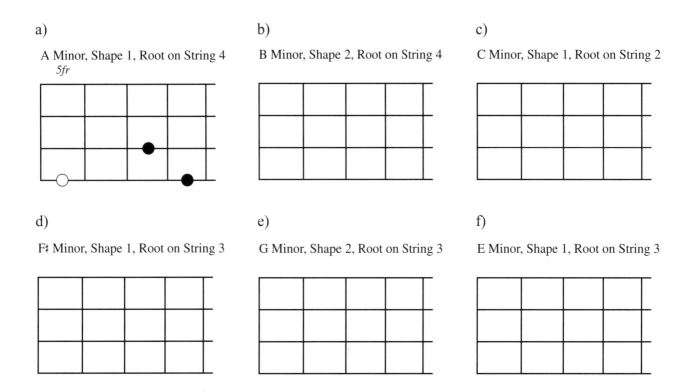

a)

A Minor, Shape 1, Root on String 4
5fr

b)

B Minor, Shape 2, Root on String 4

c)

C Minor, Shape 1, Root on String 2

d)

F♯ Minor, Shape 1, Root on String 3

e)

G Minor, Shape 2, Root on String 3

f)

E Minor, Shape 1, Root on String 3

AUGMENTED TRIAD (1–3–♯5)

The augmented triad is not nearly as common as the major and minor, but you still do see it regularly. It's like a major triad, but the 5th is raised a half step. So, to form a C augmented triad, for example, we start with the C major scale (C–D–E–F–G–A–B), take the first, third, and fifth notes (C–E–G), and then raise the 5th by a half step.

So a C augmented triad would be spelled **C–E–G♯**. Its formula is **1–3–♯5**, or **root, 3rd, ♯5th**.

We can also measure each note's interval from the root. If we do this, we'll find that an augmented triad contains the following:
- **Major 3rd (M3)**: from root to 3rd
- **Augmented 5th (A5)**: from root to ♯5th

Augmented Triad – Shape 1

This first moveable augmented triad shape is based off our first major scale pattern and uses the second finger on the root, which is indicated with an open circle. You'll have to stretch a bit to reach that ♯5th!

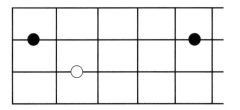

We can also move this exact shape up or down a string set to play an arpeggio from a different root note.

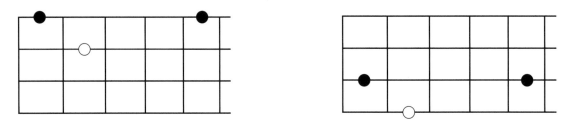

Augmented Triad – Shape 2

Our second shape is based off our alternative pattern for the major scale and uses the third or fourth finger on the root.

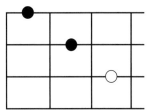

Since this shape uses three adjacent strings, we can't move it up a string set. But we can move it down a string set with the root on the fourth string.

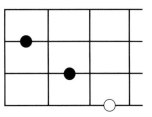

QUIZ 17

1. What is the formula for an augmented triad? _____

2. Spell the following triads. (Remember, you're just using the first, third, and fifth notes of each root's respective major scale and then raising the fifth by a half step.)

a) A augmented: _____
b) D augmented: _____
c) D♭ augmented: _____
d) E♭ augmented: _____

3. Write diagrams for the following triad arpeggios on the fretboard. Use an open circle to indicate the root, and use a fret marker to indicate position. Be sure to place the root note on the specified string and use the specified shape. The first example is done for you.

a)

G Augmented, Shape 1, Root on String 3
9fr

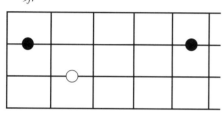

b)

E Augmented, Shape 1, Root on String 2

c)

C Augmented, Shape 2, Root on String 4

d)

A♭ Augmented, Shape 2, Root on String 3

e)

B♭ Augmented, Shape 1, Root on String 4

f)

D Augmented, Shape 2, Root on String 3

DIMINISHED TRIAD (1–♭3–♭5)

The diminished triad is not very common, but you still do see it on occasion. It's like a minor triad, but the 5th is lowered a half step. So, to form a C diminished triad, for example, we start with the C minor scale (C–D–E♭–F–G–A♭–B♭), take the first, third, and fifth notes (C–E♭–G), and then lower the 5th by a half step.

So a C diminished triad would be spelled **C–E♭–G♭**. Its formula is **1–♭3–♭5**, or **root, ♭3rd, ♭5th**.

We can also measure each note's interval from the root. If we do this, we'll find that an diminished triad contains the following:

- **Minor 3rd (m3)**: from root to ♭3rd
- **Diminished 5th (d5)**: from root to ♭5th

Diminished Triad - Shape 1

This first moveable diminished triad shape is based off our first minor scale pattern and uses the first finger on the root, which is indicated with an open circle.

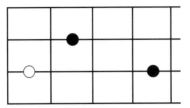

We can also move this exact shape up or down a string set to play an arpeggio from a different root note.

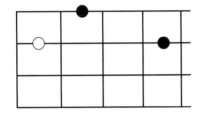
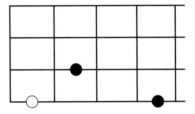

Diminished Triad - Shape 2

Our second shape is based off our alternative pattern for the major scale and uses the third finger on the root. Note that this Shape 2 is different than those of the major, minor, and augmented arpeggios in that it's played on two strings instead of three. (The ♭5th would result in quite a stretch otherwise.)

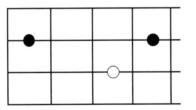

We can also move this exact shape up or down a string set to play an arpeggio from a different root note.

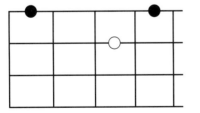
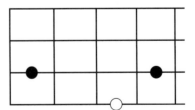

QUIZ 18

1. What is the formula for a diminished triad? _____

2. Spell the following triads. (Remember, you're just using the first, third, and fifth notes of each root's respective minor scale and then lowering the fifth by a half step.)

a) A diminished: _____
b) D diminished: _____
c) C♯ diminished: _____
d) F♯ diminished: _____

3. Write diagrams for the following triad arpeggios on the fretboard. Use an open circle to indicate the root, and use a fret marker to indicate position. Be sure to place the root note on the specified string and use the specified shape. The first example is done for you.

a)

A Diminished, Shape 1, Root on String 4
5fr

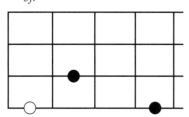

b)

C Diminished, Shape 1, Root on String 2

c)

G Diminished, Shape 2, Root on String 3

d)

E Diminished, Shape 2, Root on String 4

e)

B Diminished, Shape 1, Root on String 2

f)

G♯ Diminished, Shape 1, Root on String 4

ADDING THE OCTAVE

We can expand on all of these shapes by adding the octave on top, which will result in a root–3rd–5th–root (octave) formula for each. Some of these shapes may require you to roll a fretting finger to cover the same fret on two adjacent strings. If you've not yet become adept at this important technique, now is a good time.

Major, Shape 1 with Added Octave

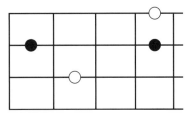

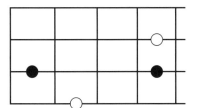

Major Shape 2 with Added Octave

The shape based off the third-string root here requires a quick shift in position to reach the octave, but it's a good one to master. The shape based off the fourth-string root can be played in all one position using all four strings.

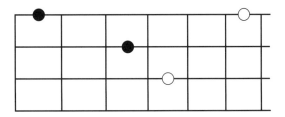

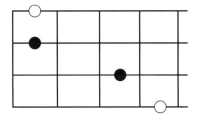

Minor Shape 1 with Added Octave

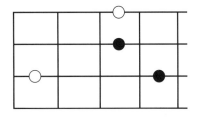

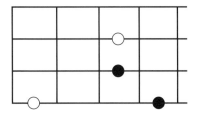

Minor Shape 2 with Added Octave

The shape based off the third-string root here requires a quick shift in position to reach the octave, but it's a good one to master. The shape based off the fourth-string root can be played in all one position using all four strings.

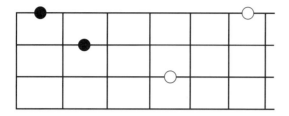
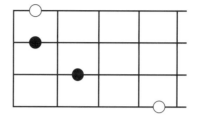

Augmented Shape 1 with Added Octave

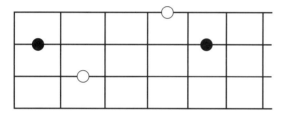
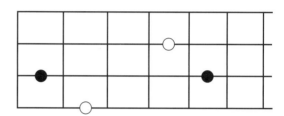

Augmented Shape 2 with Added Octave

The shape based off the third-string root here requires a quick shift in position to reach the octave, but it's a good one to master. The shape based off the fourth-string root can be played in all one position using all four strings.

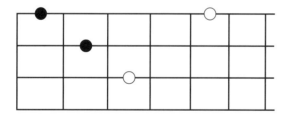
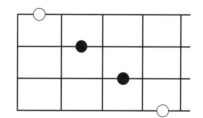

Diminished Shape 1 with Added Octave

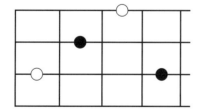
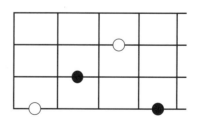

Diminished Shape 2 with Added Octave

The shape based off the third-string root here requires a slight reach to add the octave, but it's a good one to master. The shape based off the fourth-string root can be played using all four strings with just a bit of a reach.

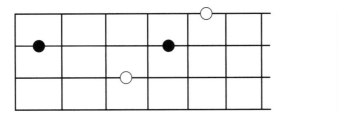 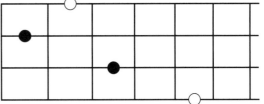

QUIZ 19

1. Write diagrams for the following triad arpeggios (with added octave) on the fretboard. Use an open circle to indicate the roots, and use a fret marker to indicate position. Be sure to place the low root note on the specified string and use the specified shape. The first example is done for you.

a)

E, Shape 1, Root on String 3

6fr

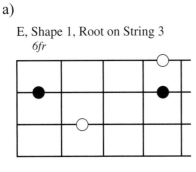

b)

Bb, Shape 2, Root on String 4

c)

D, Shape 2, Root on String 3

d)

Ab, Shape 1, Root on String 3

e)

F#m, Shape 1, Root on String 4

f)

C#m, Shape 2, Root on String 4

g)

Bm, Shape 2, Root on String 4

h)

Fm, Shape 2, Root on String 3

i)

E+, Shape 1, Root on String 3

j)

D♭+, Shape 2, Root on String 4

k)

A+, Shape 2, Root on String 3

l)

B♭+, Shape 1, Root on String 4

m)

E°, Shape 1, Root on String 3

n)

G°, Shape 1, Root on String 4

o)

F♯°, Shape 2, Root on String 3

p)

D°, Shape 2, Root on String 4

SUMMARY

Here are the things we learned in this chapter:
- A triad is a chord with three different notes: a root, a 3rd, and 5th.
- The formula for a **major triad is 1–3–5**.
- The formula for a **minor triad is 1–♭3–5**.
- The formula for an **augmented triad is 1–3–♯5**.
- The formula for a **diminished triad is 1–♭3–♭5**.
- On the bass, we normally play triads as **arpeggios**—i.e., one note at a time rather than all notes simultaneously.
- We learned two moveable shapes for each triad (major, minor, augmented, and diminished).
- We learned **chord symbols** with which to notate chords (triads):
    - "C" stands for C major
    - "Cm" stands for C minor
    - "C+" stands for C augmented
    - "C°" stands for C diminished
- We learned two moveable shapes with an added octave root on top for each triad (major, minor, augmented, and diminished).

CHAPTER 9:
OCTAVES AND ROOT POSITIONS

If you've stuck it out this far, I congratulate you. You've no doubt made a lot of progress and learned a great deal. In this chapter, we're going to piece some of the bits you've learned together and see how things overlap on the fretboard.

OCTAVES

As you know, an octave is the same note played in a higher or lower register. As bassists, we use octaves often, so we need to be familiar with how they lay out on the fretboard. Though there are many ways to play them, perhaps the most simplistic is to play a string open and then play it at the twelfth fret. The note on fret 12 is an octave higher than the open string. It's easy enough to move back and forth between those notes, but if we want to play octaves above a note other than E, A, D, and G (the notes of the open strings), we need to find another method—preferably a moveable shape that can be used anywhere on the neck.

We've actually already played moveable octave shapes several times throughout the book, but since we didn't draw attention to them, they may have not been obvious. So let's take a closer look now.

Let's say we want to play an octave above the open E string. Where could we put the higher E note? As already mentioned, we could play it on the same string at fret 12.

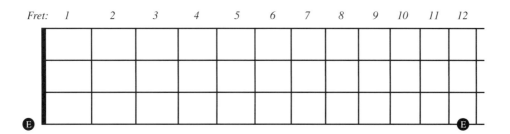

In other words, we play on the same string, only twelve frets up. The problem with this is that it's not practical when playing any notes other than the open string notes.

Where else could we put the higher E? Well, we could move it to string 3, which would be fret 7.

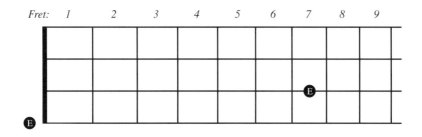

In other words, we play one string higher, seven frets up. This is closer, but it's still quite a distance to cover if the low note is not an open string.

If we move the high E note up one more string, we end up with something that's quite useful.

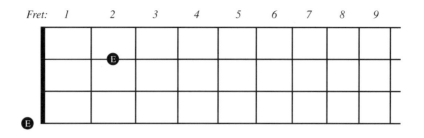

In other words, we play two strings higher, two frets up. This is more like it!

Octave Shape 1 – Fourth or Third String Root

For this shape, we use either our first or second finger for the low note and the fourth finger for the higher note.

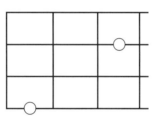

We can take this shape and move it anywhere along the fourth string to play octaves comfortably, as demonstrated below with G and B♭ octaves.

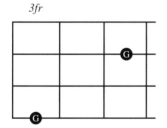
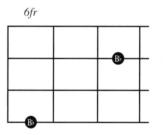

Just as with our arpeggio shapes, we can move this shape up a string set and put the root on the third string.

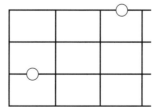

Here's what that looks like with D and F octaves.

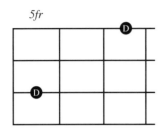 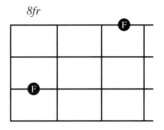

Octave Shape 2 – Fourth String Root

When the low root is on the fourth string, there's another octave shape we can use as well. This one puts your fourth finger on the low string and uses the first finger for the high note.

And here's what A and C octaves look like with that shape.

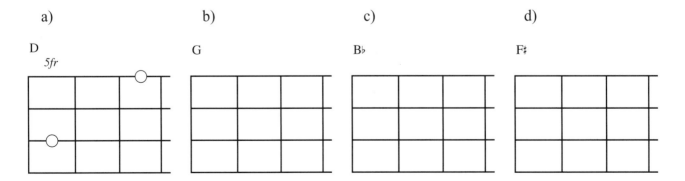

QUIZ 20

1. Write diagrams for the following octaves using shape 1 with roots on the third string. Use a fret marker to indicate position. The first example is done for you.

a)   b)   c)   d)

D   G   Bb   F♯

2. Write diagrams for the following octaves using shape 1 with roots on the fourth string. Use a fret marker to indicate position.

a)   b)   c)   d)

  A   F   B   C♯

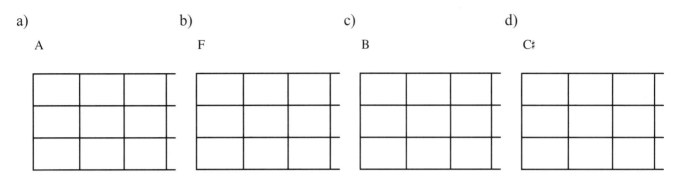

3. Write diagrams for the following octaves using shape 2 with roots on the fourth string. Use a fret marker to indicate position.

   a)   b)   c)

    C   A♭   E♭

                                    d)

                                      B

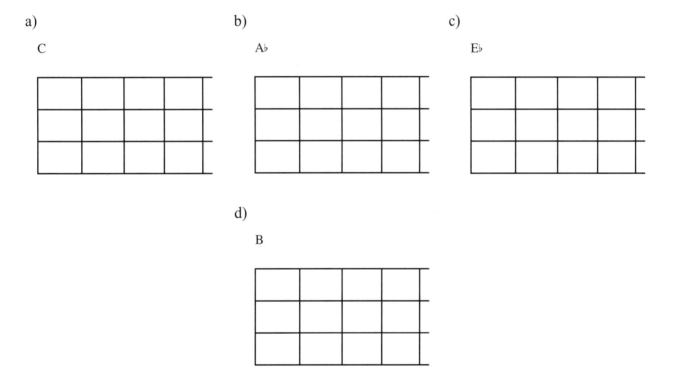

Ok, great. Now we know a few different ways to play octaves. Are they good for anything besides playing disco? They sure are. They form a framework in which you can comfortably groove. That's what we're going to look at now.

ROOT POSITIONS (GROOVE BOXES)

The great thing about octave shapes is that they form these visual boxes on the fretboard in which you can comfortably reside while laying it down. Some people call these **root positions** or **root patterns**, but I like to call them **groove boxes**. They can encompass three or four frets, depending on which finger is used on the low root note. Let's take a look at the basic idea, and later on we'll explore it a bit more.

Root on Fourth String – Second Finger on Root

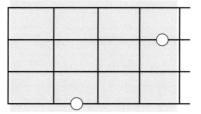

Root on Fourth String – Fourth Finger on Root

Root on Fourth String – First Finger on Root

Root on Third String – Second Finger on Root

Root on Third String – Fourth Finger on Root
In this groove box, the upper octave isn't accessible without shifting positions.

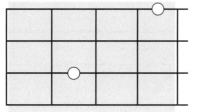

Root on Third String – First Finger on Root

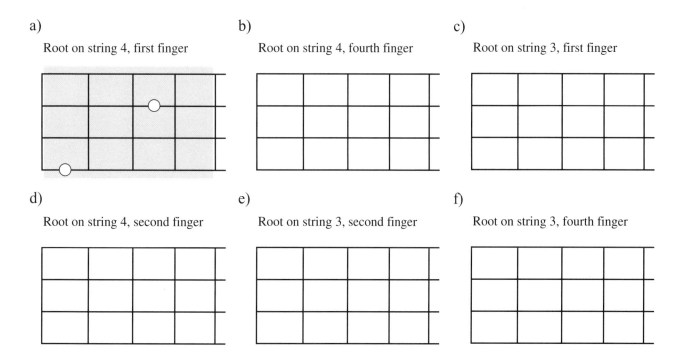

QUIZ 21

1. Draw the appropriate groove box, given the position and fingering of the low root note. The first example is done for you.

a)

Root on string 4, first finger

b)

Root on string 4, fourth finger

c)

Root on string 3, first finger

d)

Root on string 4, second finger

e)

Root on string 3, second finger

f)

Root on string 3, fourth finger

OVERLAPPING POSITIONS

Now that you're familiar with several octave shapes and root positions (groove boxes), let's see how they overlap. Becoming familiar with this idea will help you move fluidly from one position to the next on the fretboard.

Let's work with a C root as an example. Let's start with the lowest-pitched C note we have on the bass neck nearest to the nut. This is the C on string 3, fret 3.

3fr

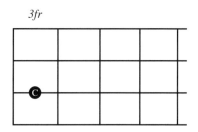

Now let's work our way up the frets, recognizing every C note along the way. Note that we're not necessarily moving up in pitch every time here; we're simply moving up in fret numbers. But we're looking for C notes on any string. The next C note would be on fret 5, string 1—an octave higher than the first one.

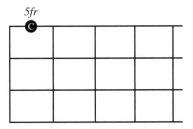

Our next C note appears at fret 8 on string 4. This is the same (low) octave as our first one.

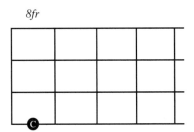

Then we have a C note at fret 10 on string 2. This is the higher octave—same as the second C.

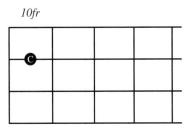

The next C we hit appears at fret 15 on string 3 and completes our journey.

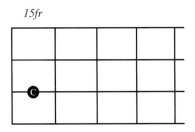

This is the same as the C we started on, only twelve frets higher up the neck. Every subsequent C note would be a repeat, only adding twelve frets each time.

So, putting it all together, here's what we have:

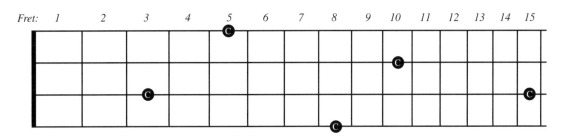

Now let's label the groove boxes and see which ones bleed into each other.

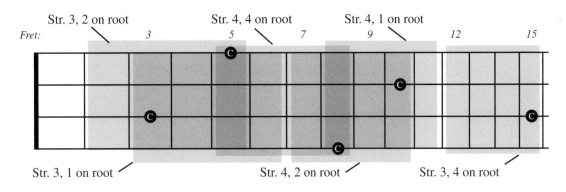

As you can see, you're never very far from comfortable territory once you become familiar with the various root positions. For example, we could play the same C major scale in three different places on the neck easily.

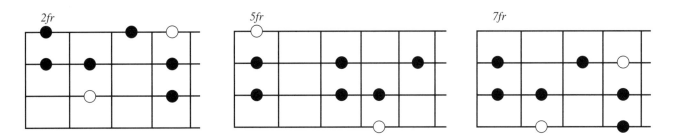

Or how about the C minor scale? Yep. It could easily be played in the same three areas.

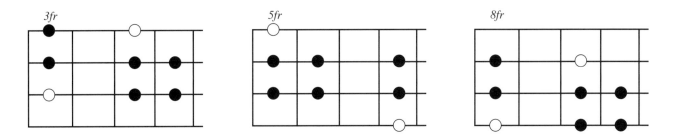

If these overlapping connections are at all unclear to you, take a moment and re-read this chapter. It's imperative that you see these connections in order to become free and roam the neck at will.

QUIZ 22

1. Draw in the overlapping root positions for the following notes spanning from the lowest possible position on the neck to twelve frets above. The first example is done for you.

a)

D root notes

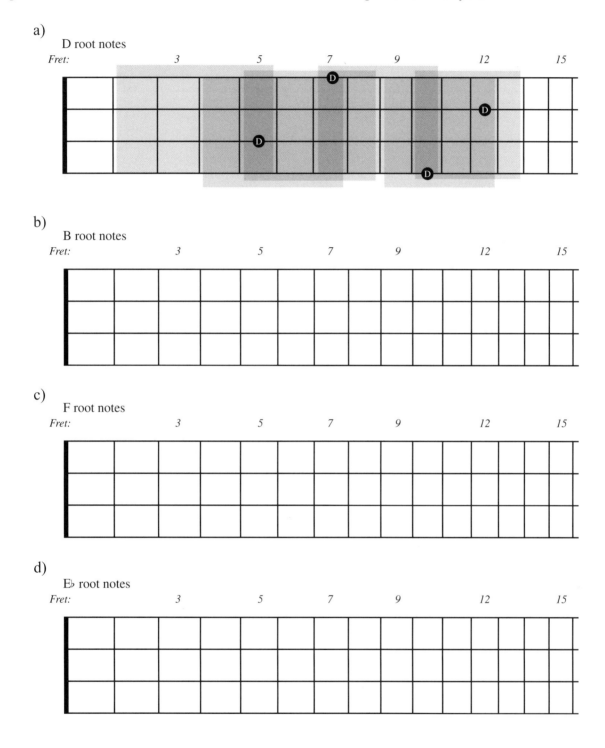

b)

B root notes

c)

F root notes

d)

E♭ root notes

SUMMARY

Here are the things we learned in this chapter:

- An **octave** is the distance of one note to the same note twelve half steps higher or lower in pitch.
- On the bass, the easiest shape for fingering the octave involves the low note appearing two frets and two strings below the higher; for example, a C note is found at fret 3, string 3, whereas one an octave higher is found at fret 5, string 1. (Remember! When talking about higher or lower strings, we're referencing the pitch—not physical space.)
- We learned two different octave shapes: Shape 1 with a low root on either string 3 or 4, and Shape 2 with a low root on string 4.
- A root position, or groove box, is an area on the neck that encompasses an octave (usually) and the surrounding notes accessible within that fingering position.
- On the bass, we generally use six different root positions: three with low roots on string 3, and three with low roots on string 4.
- Several of these root positions will overlap, covering nearly every fret within the span of an octave. Once the octave is reached (the span of twelve frets), the pattern begins to repeat.

CHAPTER 10:
PENTATONIC SCALES

A pentatonic scale, as its name ("penta" "tonic") implies, is one that contains only five different notes. In rock, blues, and country music, pentatonic scales are arguably as common (maybe more) than major and minor scales.

There are two common pentatonic scales: major pentatonic, and minor pentatonic. They're both five-note versions of their respective major and minor scales.

THE MAJOR PENTATONIC SCALE

To create a major pentatonic scale, we simply remove the fourth and seventh notes of a major scale. To create C major pentatonic, for example, we remove the fourth (F) and seventh (B) notes of the C major scale. This leaves us with five notes: C–D–E–G–A. So, the formula for a major pentatonic scale is 1–2–3–5–6.

C Major Pentatonic Scale (Second Finger on Root)

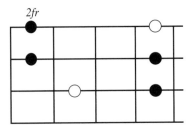

The above fingering, in second position beginning with your second finger, can be moved anywhere on the neck to play from a different tonic. It can also be moved down a string set. Playing this on string set 4–2 in second position, for example, would result in a G major pentatonic scale.

G Major Pentatonic Scale (Second Finger on Root)

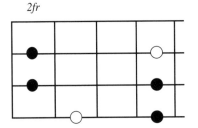

We can also play the major pentatonic scale with an alternate fingering, beginning with the fourth finger. To play a C major pentatonic scale, we'd play this shape in fifth position.

C Major Pentatonic Scale – Alternate Fingering
(Fourth Finger on Root)

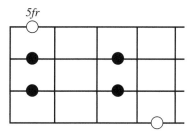

Since this fingering uses all four strings, we're not able to move the same exact shape up a string set. However, we can access all the notes except for the top octave. If we move up a string set and stay in fifth position, for example, we'll have an F major pentatonic scale.

F Major Pentatonic Scale – Alternate Fingering
(Fourth Finger on Root, Partial Pattern)

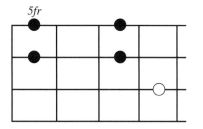

QUIZ 22

1. Draw the diagrams for the major pentatonic scales given the following information. The first example is done for you.

a)

D Major Pentatonic
(Second finger on Root, Str. 3)

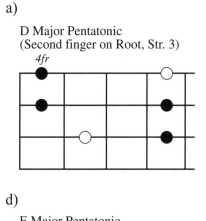

b)

E♭ Major Pentatonic
(Fourth finger on Root, Str. 4)

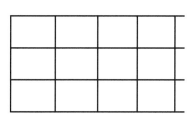

c)

A♭ Major Pentatonic
(Second finger on Root, Str. 3)

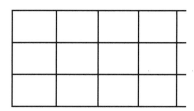

d)

F Major Pentatonic
(Second finger on Root, Str. 4)

e)

B Major Pentatonic
(Fourth finger on Root, Str. 4)

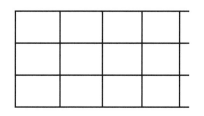

f)

E Major Pentatonic
(Fourth finger on Root, Str. 3)

THE MINOR PENTATONIC SCALE

To create a minor pentatonic scale, we remove the second and sixth notes of a minor scale. To create C minor pentatonic, for example, we remove the second (D) and sixth (A♭) notes of the C minor scale. This leaves us with five notes: C–E♭–F–G–B♭. So, the formula for a minor pentatonic scale is 1–♭3–4–5–♭7.

C Minor Pentatonic Scale (First Finger on Root)

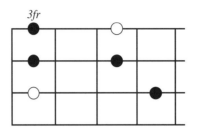

The above fingering, in third position beginning with your first finger, can be moved anywhere on the neck to play from a different tonic. It can also be moved down a string set. Playing this on string set 4–2 in second position, for example, would result in a G minor pentatonic scale.

G Minor Pentatonic Scale (First Finger on Root)

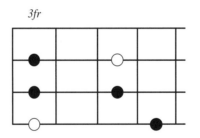

We can also play the minor pentatonic scale with an alternate fingering, beginning with the fourth finger. To play a C minor pentatonic scale, we'd play this shape in fifth position.

C Minor Pentatonic Scale – Alternate Fingering (Fourth Finger on Root)

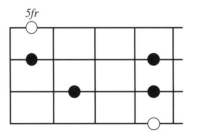

Since this fingering uses all four strings, we're not able to move the same exact shape up a string set. However, we can access all the notes except for the top octave. If we move up a string set and stay in fifth position, for example, we'll have an F minor pentatonic scale.

F Minor Pentatonic Scale – Alternate Fingering
(Fourth Finger on Root, Partial Pattern)

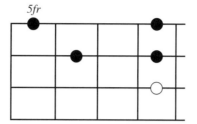

QUIZ 23

1. Draw the diagrams for the minor pentatonic scales given the following information. The first example is done for you.

a)

D Minor Pentatonic
(Fourth finger on Root, Str. 4)

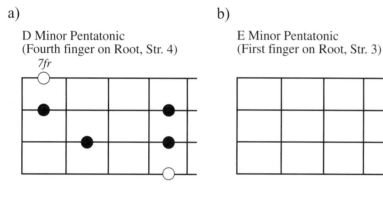

b)

E Minor Pentatonic
(First finger on Root, Str. 3)

c)

F♯ Minor Pentatonic
(First finger on Root, Str. 4)

d)

A Minor Pentatonic
(Fourth finger on Root, Str. 3)

e)

B Minor Pentatonic
(Fourth finger on Root, Str. 4)

f)

C♯ Minor Pentatonic
(First finger on Root, Str. 3)

SHIFTING FINGERINGS

There are also some common pentatonic fingerings that involve a shift in position. These are handy for moving you into a higher range on the fretboard, which allows access to more notes.

Major Pentatonic Scale – Shift Fingering

The shift fingering for the major pentatonic begins with the first finger on either the third or fourth string. Here's the C major pentatonic scale, for example, starting in third position on string 3.

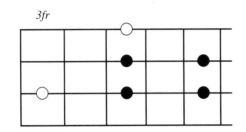

Minor Pentatonic Scale – Shift Fingering

The shift fingering for the minor pentatonic begins with the fourth finger on either the third or fourth string. Here's the C minor pentatonic scale, for example, starting with the fourth finger on fret 8, string 4.

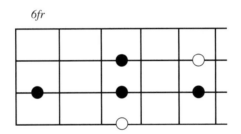

Again, both of these fingerings can be moved to a different string set to play the scales from different roots.

QUIZ 24

1. Draw the shift fingering pentatonic scale patterns given the following information. The first example is done for you.

a)

D Major Pentatonic (Root on Str. 3)

b)

F Major Pentatonic (Root on Str. 4)

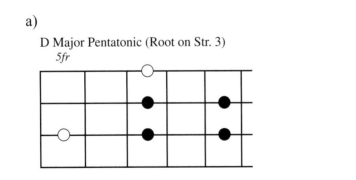

c)

E Minor Pentatonic (Root on Str. 3)

d)

F Minor Pentatonic (Root on Str. 4)

e)

G♯ Major Pentatonic (Root on Str. 3)

f)

B Major Pentatonic (Root on Str. 4)

SUMMARY

Here are the things we learned in this chapter:

- A **pentatonic scale** contains five different notes.
- The **major pentatonic scale** contains the notes of a major scale minus the fourth and seventh notes; its formula is 1–2–3–5–6.
- The **minor pentatonic scale** contains the notes of a minor scale minus the second and sixth notes; its formula is 1–♭3–4–5–♭7.
- We learned two different fingerings for each (major and minor pentatonic) that remain in one position.
- We also learned a shift fingering for each (major and minor pentatonic), which shifts up two frets at some point, allowing access to higher notes.

CHAPTER 11:
SEVENTH CHORDS

In chapter 8, we learned how to play several triads as arpeggios in different fingering patterns. In this chapter, we're going to extend that concept to **seventh chords**. Whereas triads contain three different notes, seventh chords contain four different notes.

Remember how we "stacked 3rds" to build triads? With a seventh chord, we continue that process and stack one more 3rd on top. There are several different qualities of seventh chords we'll learn here, and for each one, we essentially use the same process that we did for triads—i.e., stacking 3rds and altering notes as necessary to adhere to the formula for each.

MAJOR SEVENTH CHORDS (1-3-5-7)

The major seventh chord is similar to the major triad (1–3–5), but it has an added 7th on top. These are built simply by using the first, third, fifth, and seventh notes of a major scale. To build a C major seventh chord, for example, we'll use every other note of that scale.

C – D – **E** – F – **G** – A – **B**

Since we didn't alter any of these notes, we didn't stray from the major scale formula. So we can say the formula for a major seventh chord is 1–3–5–7, or root–3rd–5th–7th.

We can also measure each note's interval from the root. If we do this, we'll find that a major seventh chord contains the following:
- **Major 3rd (M3)**: from root to 3rd
- **Perfect 5th (P5)**: from root to 5th
- **Major 7th (M7)**: from root to 7th

Just as triads do, seventh chords have shorthand symbols as well. The chord symbol for a major seventh chord is the letter followed by "maj7."

Major Seventh – Shape 1

So let's take a look at some moveable shapes for a major seventh chord. This first one is based off our first major scale pattern and uses the second finger on the root, which is indicated with an open circle.

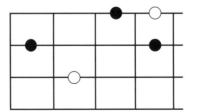

We can also move this exact shape down a string set to play an arpeggio from a different root note.

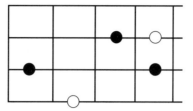

Major Seventh – Shape 2

Our second shape begins with the first finger and includes a position shift. It's somewhat similar to the major pentatonic shift fingering.

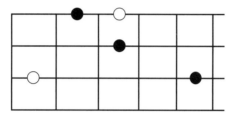

We can also move it down a string set with the root on the fourth string.

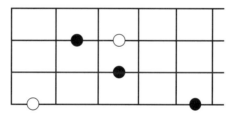

QUIZ 25

1. How many notes are in a seventh chord? _____

2. What is the formula for a major seventh? _____

3. Spell the following major seventh chords. (Remember, you're just using the first, third, fifth, and seventh notes of each root's respective major scale. So you'll need to spell the major scale first, if necessary.)

    a) Amaj7: _____
    b) Dmaj7: _____
    c) Bmaj7: _____
    d) Fmaj7: _____

4. Write diagrams for the following major seventh arpeggios on the fretboard. Use an open circle to indicate the roots, and use a fret marker to indicate position. Be sure to place the low root note on the specified string and use the specified shape. The first example is done for you.

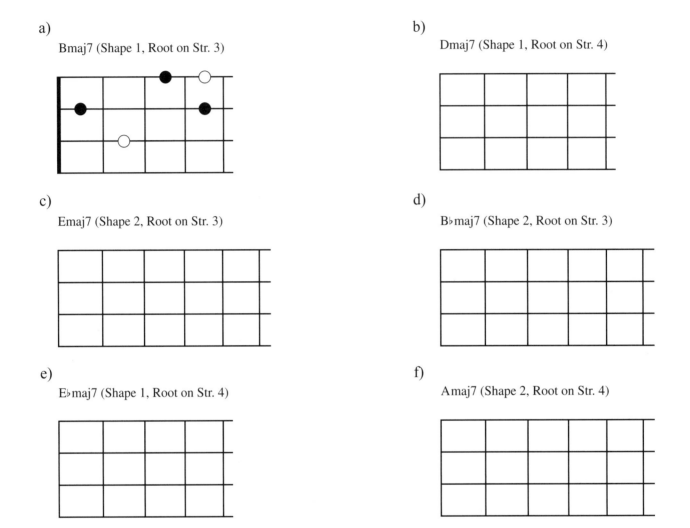

a)

Bmaj7 (Shape 1, Root on Str. 3)

b)

Dmaj7 (Shape 1, Root on Str. 4)

c)

Emaj7 (Shape 2, Root on Str. 3)

d)

B♭maj7 (Shape 2, Root on Str. 3)

e)

E♭maj7 (Shape 1, Root on Str. 4)

f)

Amaj7 (Shape 2, Root on Str. 4)

MINOR SEVENTH CHORDS (1–♭3–5–♭7)

The minor seventh chord is similar to the minor triad (1–♭3–5), but it has an added ♭7th on top. These are built simply by using the first, third, fifth, and seventh notes of a minor scale. To build a C minor seventh chord, for example, we'll use every other note of that scale.

C – D – E♭ – F – G – A♭ – B♭

So we can say the formula for a minor seventh chord is 1–♭3–5–♭7, or root–♭3rd–5th–♭7th.

We can also measure each note's interval from the root. If we do this, we'll find that a minor seventh chord contains the following:
- **Minor 3rd (m3)**: from root to ♭3rd
- **Perfect 5th (P5)**: from root to 5th
- **Minor 7th (m7)**: from root to ♭7th

The chord symbol for a minor seventh chord is the letter followed by "m7."

Minor Seventh – Shape 1

So let's take a look at some moveable shapes for a minor seventh chord. This first one is based off our first minor scale pattern and uses the first finger on the root, which is indicated with an open circle.

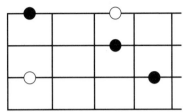

We can also move this exact shape down a string set to play an arpeggio from a different root note.

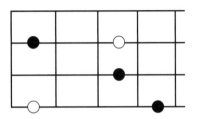

Minor Seventh – Shape 2

Our second shape begins with the fourth finger. It's somewhat similar to the minor pentatonic alternate fingering. Note that, since this fingering uses all four strings, it can't be moved to a different string set. (Though you could move it up a string set to play an incomplete m7 arpeggio. You'd be able to access all the notes without a position shift except for the high root.)

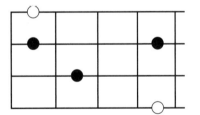

QUIZ 26

1. What is the formula for a minor seventh? _____

2. Spell the following minor seventh chords. (Remember, you're just using the first, third, fifth, and seventh notes of each root's respective minor scale. So you'll need to spell the minor scale first, if necessary.)

    a) Am7: _____
    b) Dm7: _____
    c) Bm7: _____
    d) Fm7: _____

3. Write diagrams for the following minor seventh arpeggios on the fretboard. Use an open circle to indicate the roots, and use a fret marker to indicate position. Be sure to place the low root note on the specified string and use the specified shape. The first example is done for you.

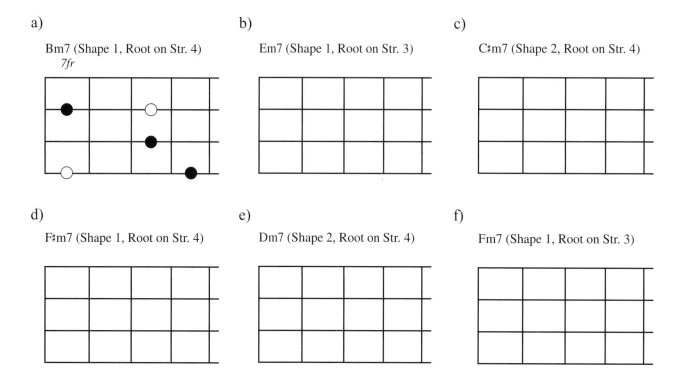

a)
Bm7 (Shape 1, Root on Str. 4)

b)
Em7 (Shape 1, Root on Str. 3)

c)
C#m7 (Shape 2, Root on Str. 4)

d)
F#m7 (Shape 1, Root on Str. 4)

e)
Dm7 (Shape 2, Root on Str. 4)

f)
Fm7 (Shape 1, Root on Str. 3)

DOMINANT SEVENTH CHORDS (1–3–5–♭7)

The dominant seventh chord is similar to the major triad (1–3–5), but it has an added ♭7th on top. These are built simply by using the first, third, fifth, and seventh notes of a major scale and lowering the 7th by one half step. To build a C dominant seventh chord, for example, we'll use every other note of the major scale and flat the seventh tone.

C – D – E – F – G – A – B♭

So we can say the formula for a dominant seventh chord is 1–♭3–5–♭7, or root–♭3rd–5th–♭7th.

We can also measure each note's interval from the root. If we do this, we'll find that a dominant seventh chord contains the following:
- **Major 3rd (M3)**: from root to 3rd
- **Perfect 5th (P5)**: from root to 5th
- **Minor 7th (m7)**: from root to ♭7th

The chord symbol for a dominant seventh chord is the letter followed by "7."

Dominant Seventh – Shape 1

So let's take a look at some moveable shapes for a dominant seventh chord. This first one is based off our first major scale pattern and uses the second finger on the root, which is indicated with an open circle.

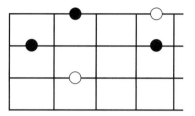

We can also move this exact shape down a string set to play an arpeggio from a different root note.

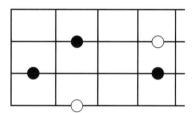

Dominant Seventh – Shape 2

Our second shape begins with the fourth finger and is somewhat similar to the alternative major scale pattern. Note that, since this fingering uses all four strings, it can't be moved to a different string set. (Though you could move it up a string set to play an incomplete dominant seventh arpeggio. You'd be able to access all the notes without a position shift except for the high root.)

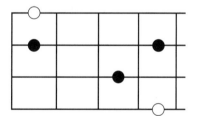

QUIZ 27

1. What is the formula for a dominant seventh? _____

2. Spell the following dominant seventh chords. (Remember, you're just using the first, third, fifth, and flat seventh notes of each root's respective major scale. So you'll need to spell the major scale first, if necessary.)

    a) A7: _____
    b) D7: _____
    c) B7: _____
    d) F7: _____

3. Write diagrams for the following dominant seventh arpeggios on the fretboard. Use an open circle to indicate the roots, and use a fret marker to indicate position. Be sure to place the low root note on the specified string and use the specified shape. The first example is done for you.

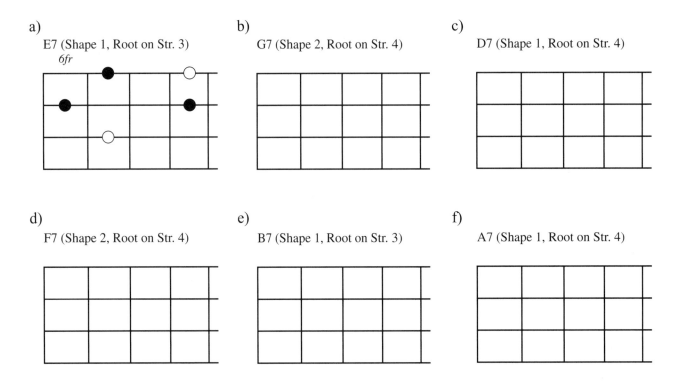

a)
E7 (Shape 1, Root on Str. 3)

b)
G7 (Shape 2, Root on Str. 4)

c)
D7 (Shape 1, Root on Str. 4)

d)
F7 (Shape 2, Root on Str. 4)

e)
B7 (Shape 1, Root on Str. 3)

f)
A7 (Shape 1, Root on Str. 4)

MINOR SEVENTH FLAT FIVE CHORDS (1–♭3–♭5–♭7)

The minor seventh flat five chord is similar to the minor triad (1–♭3–5), but it has a lowered 5th and an added ♭7th on top. These are built simply by using the first, third, fifth, and seventh notes of a minor scale and lowering the fifth note by a half step. To build a C minor seventh flat five chord, for example, we'll use every other note of that scale and lower the fifth note.

C – D – E♭ – F – G♭ – A♭ – B♭

So we can say the formula for a minor seventh flat five chord is 1–♭3–♭5–♭7, or root–♭3rd–♭5th–♭7th.

We can also measure each note's interval from the root. If we do this, we'll find that a minor seventh flat five chord contains the following:
- **Minor 3rd (m3)**: from root to ♭3rd
- **Diminished 5th (d5)**: from root to ♭5th
- **Minor 7th (m7)**: from root to ♭7th

The chord symbol for a minor seventh flat five chord is the letter followed by "m7♭5."

Minor Seventh Flat Five – Shape 1

So let's take a look at some moveable shapes for a minor seventh flat five chord. This first one is based off our first minor scale pattern and uses the first finger on the root, which is indicated with an open circle.

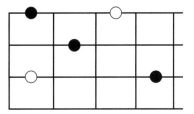

We can also move this exact shape down a string set to play an arpeggio from a different root note.

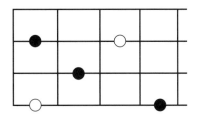

Minor Seventh Flat Five – Shape 2

Our second shape begins with the third or fourth finger and contains a quick position shift.

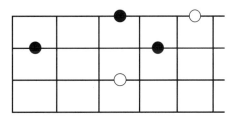

We can also move this exact shape down a string set to play an arpeggio from a different root note.

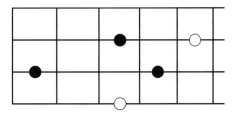

QUIZ 28

1. What is the formula for a minor seventh flat five? _____

2. Spell the following minor seventh flat five chords. (Remember, you're just using the first, third, fifth, and seventh notes of each root's respective minor scale and lowering the fifth note by a half step. So you'll need to spell the minor scale first, if necessary.) Watch out for the last one; it's a bit tricky!

    a) Am7♭5: _____
    b) Dm7♭5: _____
    c) Bm7♭5: _____
    d) Fm7♭5: _____

3. Write diagrams for the following minor seventh flat five arpeggios on the fretboard. Use an open circle to indicate the roots, and use a fret marker to indicate position. Be sure to place the low root note on the specified string and use the specified shape. The first example is done for you.

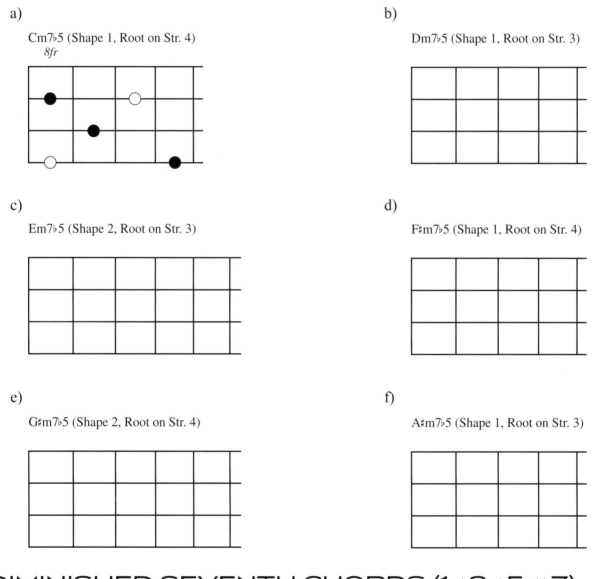

a)

    Cm7♭5 (Shape 1, Root on Str. 4)
        8fr

b)

    Dm7♭5 (Shape 1, Root on Str. 3)

c)

    Em7♭5 (Shape 2, Root on Str. 3)

d)

    F♯m7♭5 (Shape 1, Root on Str. 4)

e)

    G♯m7♭5 (Shape 2, Root on Str. 4)

f)

    A♯m7♭5 (Shape 1, Root on Str. 3)

DIMINISHED SEVENTH CHORDS (1–♭3–♭5–♭♭7)

The diminished seventh chord is similar to the minor triad (1–♭3–5), but it has a lowered 5th and an added ♭♭7th on top. You read right: a ♭♭7th. This means that, instead of just lowering the seventh note by a half step, we actually lower it by a whole step. To build a C diminished seventh chord, for example, we'll use every other note of a C minor scale, lower the fifth note by a half step, and lower the seventh note by another half step to ♭♭7th.

C – D – **E**♭ – F – **G**♭ – A♭ – **B**♭♭

So we can say the formula for a diminished seventh chord is 1→♭3→♭5→♭♭7, or root→♭3rd→♭5th→♭♭7th.

We can also measure each note's interval from the root. If we do this, we'll find that a diminished seventh chord contains the following:
- **Minor 3rd (m3)**: from root to ♭3rd
- **Diminished 5th (d5)**: from root to ♭5th
- **Diminished 7th (d7)**: from root to ♭♭7th

The chord symbol for a diminished seventh chord is the letter followed by "°7."

There are a few peculiar things about the diminished seventh chord. First of all, if you look closely at the ♭♭7th note, you'll notice that it's a B♭♭ note. This is one half step lower than the note B♭, which means it's actually the same at the note A. In other words, B♭♭ is enharmonic to A. So why don't we call it an A? Well, if we called it an A, the formula would be 1→♭3→♭5–6, and the formula is supposed to be 1→♭3→♭5→♭♭7. It's the same reason we call C to D♯ an augmented 2nd interval instead of a minor 3rd; even though they're the same amount of half steps (three), there are two note names involved (C and D), so the interval has to be some kind of 2nd.

The other interesting thing about this chord is that it's symmetrical. Examine it closely, and you'll find that each note in the chord is a minor 3rd (or three half steps) apart.

- C to E♭ is a minor 3rd.
- E♭ to G♭ is a minor 3rd.
- G♭ to B♭♭ is a minor 3rd.
- B♭♭ to C is (technically) an augmented 2nd, which is the same (sound-wise) as a minor 3rd.

Diminished seventh – Shape 1
So let's take a look at some moveable shapes for a diminished seventh chord. This first one is based off our first minor scale pattern and uses the first finger on the root, which is indicated with an open circle. This one does contain one position shift though.

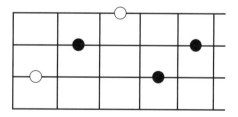

We can also move this exact shape down a string set to play an arpeggio from a different root note.

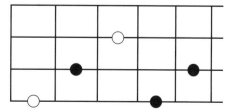

Diminished seventh – Shape 2

Our second shape begins with the third or fourth finger and also contains a position shift.

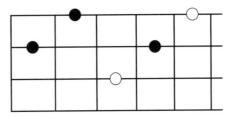

We can also move this exact shape down a string set to play an arpeggio from a different root note.

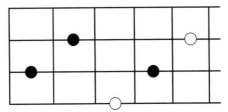

QUIZ 29

1. What is the formula for a diminished seventh? _____

2. Spell the following diminished seventh chords. (Remember, you're just using the first, third, fifth, and seventh notes of each root's respective minor scale and lowering the fifth and seventh notes by a half step. So you'll need to spell the minor scale first, if necessary.) Watch out for the last one; it's a bit tricky!

    a) A°7: _____
    b) D°7: _____
    c) B°7: _____
    d) F#°7: _____

3. Write diagrams for the following diminished seventh arpeggios on the fretboard. Use an open circle to indicate the roots, and use a fret marker to indicate position. Be sure to place the low root note on the specified string and use the specified shape. The first example is done for you.

a)

C#°7 (Shape 1, Root on Str. 3)

b)

D°7 (Shape 2, Root on Str. 4)

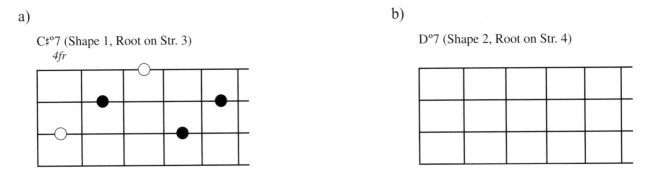

c)

E°7 (Shape 2, Root on Str. 3)

d)

G°7 (Shape 1, Root on Str. 4)

e)

B°7 (Shape 2, Root on Str. 4)

f)

F♯°7 (Shape 1, Root on Str. 3)

"CHORD"IALLY SPEAKING

Interestingly, when referring in non-specific terms—such as, "Here are the seventh chords in the key of C"—we use the term "seventh." However, often times when the chord symbols are read, we say "seven" instead of "seventh."

For example, Cmaj7 is often read aloud as "C major seven" instead of "C major seventh." Bm7♭5 is often read aloud as "B minor seven flat five" instead of "B minor seventh flat five."

This isn't a steadfast rule, and you do hear some people say "C major seventh." But the use of "seven" in chord names is arguably more popular.

SUMMARY

Here are the things we learned in this chapter:
- A seventh chord contains four different notes: a root, a 3rd, a 5th, and a 7th.
- The formula for a **major seventh chord is 1–3–5–7.**
- The formula for a **minor seventh chord is 1–♭3–5–♭7.**
- The formula for a **dominant seventh chord is 1–3–5–♭7.**
- The formula for a **minor seventh flat five chord is 1–♭3–♭5–♭7.**
- The formula for a **diminished seventh chord is 1–♭3–♭5–♭♭7.**
- On the bass, we normally play seventh chords as **arpeggios**—i.e., one note at a time rather than all notes simultaneously.
- We learned two moveable shapes for each seventh chord (major, minor, dominant, minor seven flat five, and diminished).
- We learned **chord symbols** with which to notate these seventh chords:
  - "Cmaj7" stands for C major seven
  - "Cm7" stands for C minor seven
  - "C7" stands for C dominant seven (or simply "C seven")
  - "Cm7♭5" stands for C minor seven flat five
  - "C°7" stands for C diminished seven
- We learned two moveable shapes with an added octave root on top for each seventh chord (major, minor, dominant, minor seven flat five, and diminished).

CONCLUSION

We've covered a lot of ground in this book, and your understanding of the fretboard should be broadened in every way. Be sure to reread the chapters that didn't fully make sense the first time; I'm sure the information will sink in with repeated exposure. To summarize, here's a final list of topics with which you should be familiar after working through this book:

- The **principals of the musical alphabet**, including the seven letter names used and the **location of the natural half steps**.
- The notes on each string of the bass progress up the fretboard the same way they do on a piano from left to right.
- A flat note is one fret lower than a natural note; a sharp note is one fret higher.
- The **workings of intervals**, including whole steps and half steps, as well as all possible intervals within the octave.
- The **major scale intervallic formula** of whole–whole–half–whole–whole–whole–half and **its numeric formula** of 1–2–3–4–5–6–7 (no alterations).
- The starting note of a scale is referred to as the **tonic** (or sometimes **root**).
- Two notes that sound the same but are spelled differently are **enharmonic**.
- Intervals consist of a **quantity** and a **quality**. The five qualities possible for an interval are **major**, **minor**, **augmented**, **diminished**, and **perfect**.
- Fretboard shapes for every possible interval within the octave using moveable shapes that can be moved up or down the neck and sometimes up or down a string set to play from different roots.
- The **numeric formula for a minor scale** of 1–2–♭3–4–5–♭6–♭7 and **its intervallic formula** of whole–half–whole–whole–half–whole–whole.
- Formulas for the following triads: **major**, **minor**, **augmented**, and **diminished**.
- Formulas for the following seventh chords: **major seventh**, **minor seventh**, **dominant seventh**, **minor seventh flat five**, and **diminished seventh**.
- Several moveable patterns for the following scales: **major**, **minor**, **major pentatonic**, **minor pentatonic**.
- Several **root positions**, or "**groove boxes**," that surround various scale patterns and allow you to see connections between different positions.

There are many details within this list as well, and, assuming you aced all the quizzes, you should be familiar with them as well. If not, take as much time as you need reviewing the weak areas until it all makes sense.

It's vital to remember that all of this information only truly becomes valuable when applied in your studies. So make a concerted effort to use this stuff. Try playing your favorite bass lines in different areas of the neck and with different fingerings. You're now equipped with the skills to figure out how to do things like this. Try figuring out intervals that you hear in bass lines or melodies. Try playing bass lines or melodies over songs you hear (or make up your own) using the scale patterns you've learned. Some of this may take you awhile, but once you've worked through this book, you **can** do it. It will all get quicker with increased experience.

And there's no reason to stop here. You've taken a leap forward with your knowledge with the material in this book, but there are still many more musical mountains to climb. Now that you know how the bass fretboard works, you'll have the map with which to climb them. I hope you've enjoyed working through this book with me, and I wish you the best of luck in the future.

APPENDIX

ANSWER KEY

Quiz 1
1.

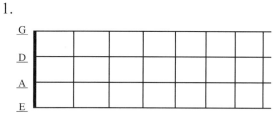

2.
    a) A
    b) G
    c) D
    d) E

Extra credit:
    a) D
    b) G
    c) E
    d) A

Quiz 2
1.
    a) F
    b) A#/Bb
    c) D
    d) F#/Gb

Quiz 3
1.
    a) D
    b) C
    c) A#/Bb
    d) F#/Gb

2.
    a) A
    b) F
    c) D#/Eb
    d) A#/Bb

Quiz 4
1.
    a) C#/Db
    b) E
    c) F#/Gb
    d) C

2.
    a) A#/Bb
    b) F
    c) F#/Gb
    d) C

Quiz 5
1.
    a) F
    b) A
    c) C#/Db
    d) A#/Bb

2.
    a) 1
    b) B
    c) F#/Gb
    d) E

Quiz 6
1.
    a) A
    b) C#/Db
    c) F
    d) D#/Eb

2.
    a) 3
    b) F#/Gb
    c) C#/Db
    d) A#/Bb

Quiz 7

1.
    a) F to G: whole step
    b) D to D♯/E♭: half step
    c) F to G: whole step
    d) E to F: half step

2.
    a) Half step
    b) Half step
    c) C♯/D♭
    d) G♯/A♭

Quiz 8

1.
    a)

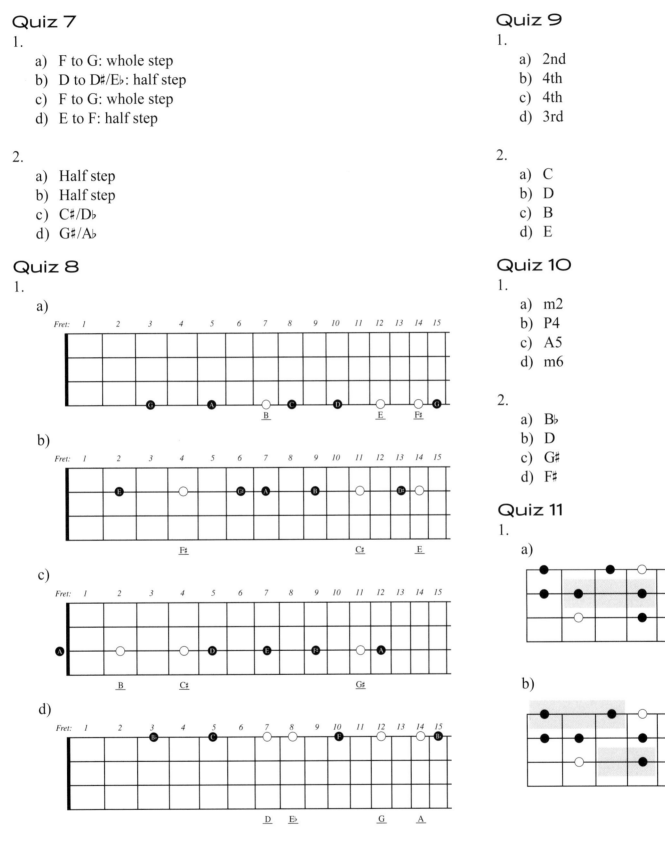

    b)

    c)

    d)

2.
    a) E–F♯–G♯–A–B–C♯–D♯–E
    b) E♭–F–G–A♭–B♭–C–D–E♭
    c) 2: B♭ and E♭
    d) 2: F♯ and C♯

Quiz 9

1.
    a) 2nd
    b) 4th
    c) 4th
    d) 3rd

2.
    a) C
    b) D
    c) B
    d) E

Quiz 10

1.
    a) m2
    b) P4
    c) A5
    d) m6

2.
    a) B♭
    b) D
    c) G♯
    d) F♯

Quiz 11

1.
    a)

    b)

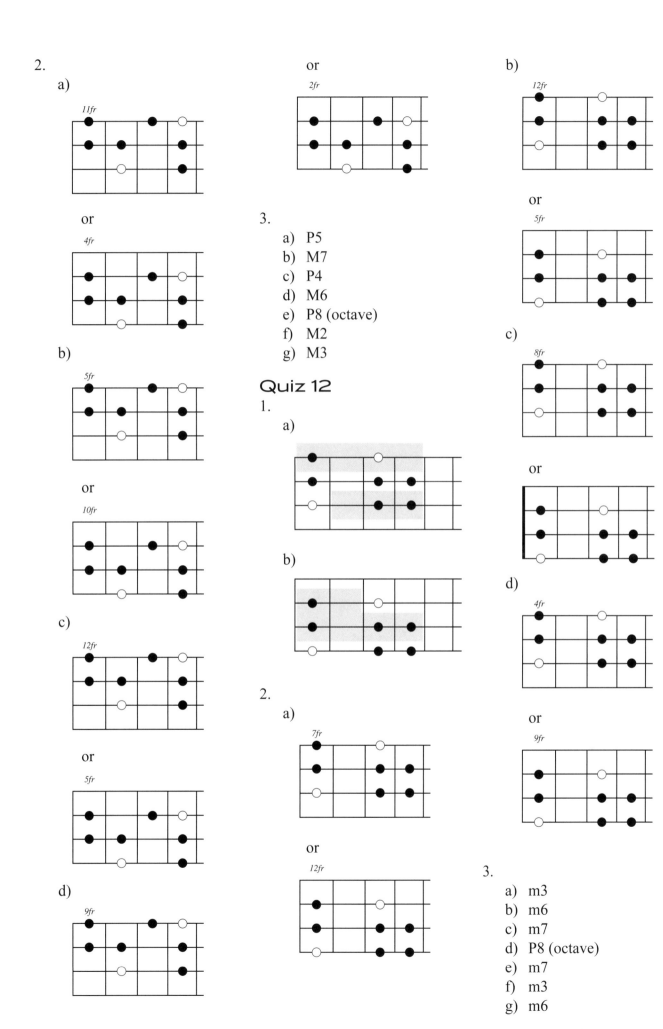

2.
a) *11fr*

or
4fr

b) *5fr*

or
10fr

c) *12fr*

or
5fr

d) *9fr*

or
2fr

3.
a) P5
b) M7
c) P4
d) M6
e) P8 (octave)
f) M2
g) M3

Quiz 12
1.
a)

b)

2.
a) *7fr*

or
12fr

b) *12fr*

or
5fr

c) *8fr*

or

d) *4fr*

or
9fr

3.
a) m3
b) m6
c) m7
d) P8 (octave)
e) m7
f) m3
g) m6

Quiz 13

1.
  a) A4 or d5
  b) m3 or A2
  c) m6 or A5
  d) m2
  e) M7
  f) M2
  g) M3

2.
  a)

P4

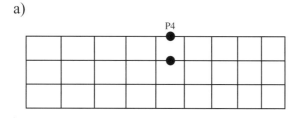

  b)

A5

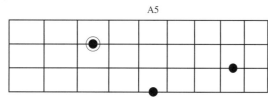

  c)

m2

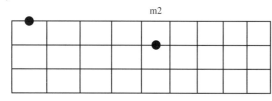

  d)

m3

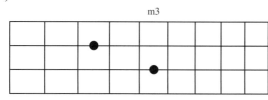

  e)

m7

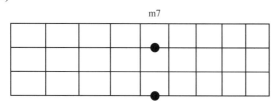

f)

M6

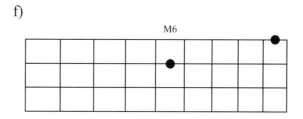

g)

d5

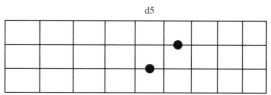

h)

A2

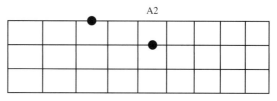

Extra credit:
  b)
  c)
  d)
  e)

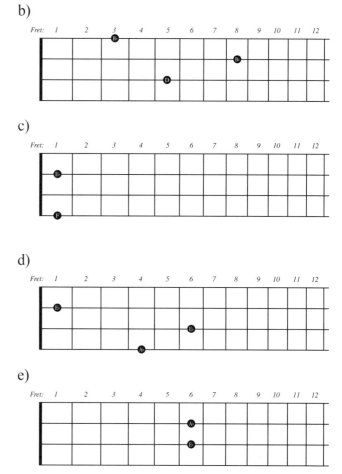

f)

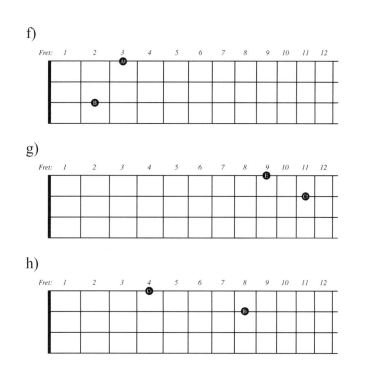

g)

h)

Quiz 14
1.

b)

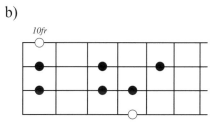

c)

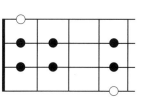

d)

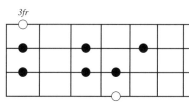

e)

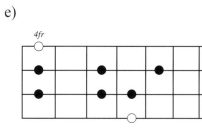

f)

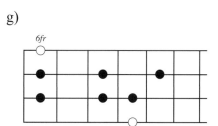

g)

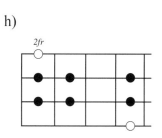

h)

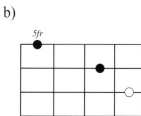

Quiz 15
1. 3

2. 1–3–5

3.

    a) A–C♯–E
    b) D–F♯–A
    c) B♭–D–F
    d) F–A–C

4.

b)

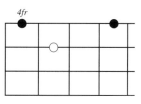

c)

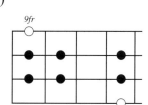

d)

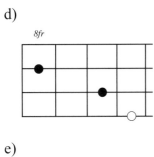

8fr

d)

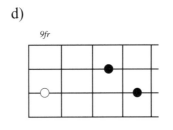

9fr

d)

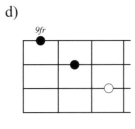

9fr

e)

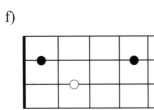

5fr

e)

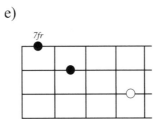

7fr

e)

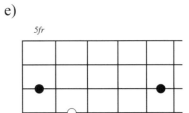

5fr

f)

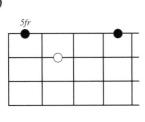

f)

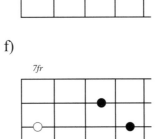

7fr

f)

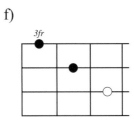

3fr

Quiz 16
1. 1–♭3–5

2.
    a) A–C–E
    b) D–F–A
    c) C♯–E–G♯
    d) F♯–A–C♯

3.
    b)

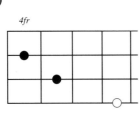

4fr

    c)

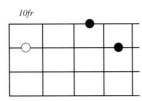

10fr

Quiz 17
1. 1–3–♯5

2.
    a) A–C♯–E♯
    b) D–F♯–A♯
    c) D♭–F–A
    d) E♭–G–B

3.
    b)

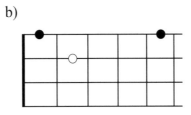

    c)

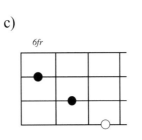

6fr

Quiz 18
1. 1–♭3–♭5

2.
    a) A–C–E♭
    b) D–F–A♭
    c) C♯–E–G
    d) F♯–A–C

3.
    b)

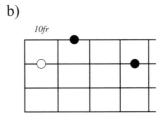

10fr

    c)

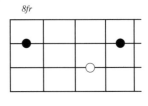

8fr

d)

10fr

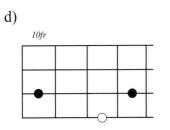

e)

9fr

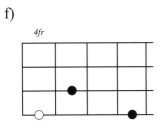

f)

4fr

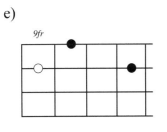

Quiz 19

1.

b)

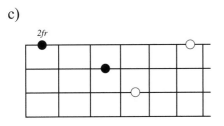

c)

2fr

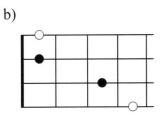

d)

10fr

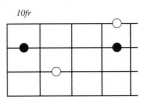

e)

2fr

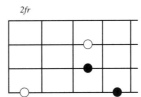

f)

6fr

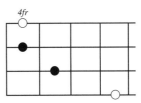

g)

4fr

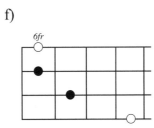

h)

5fr

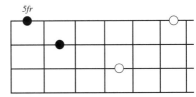

i)

6fr

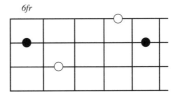

j)

6fr

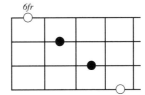

k)

10fr

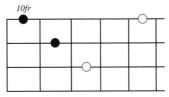

l)

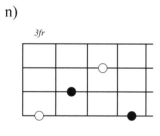
5fr

m)

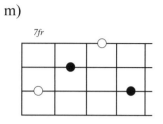
7fr

n)

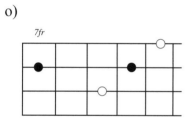
3fr

o)

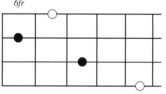
7fr

p)

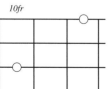
6fr

Quiz 20

1.

b)

10fr

c)

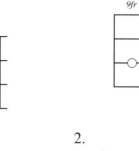

d)

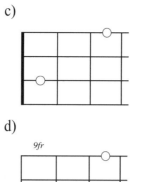
9fr

2.

a)

5fr

b)

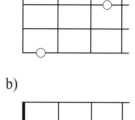

c)

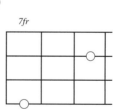
7fr

d)

9fr

3.

a)

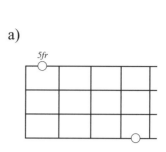
5fr

b)

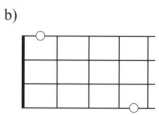

c)

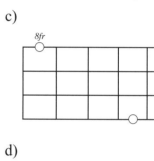
8fr

d)

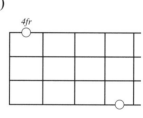
4fr

Quiz 21

1.

b)

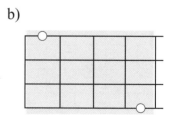

c)

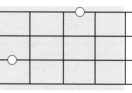

d)

e)

f)

Quiz 22

1.

b)

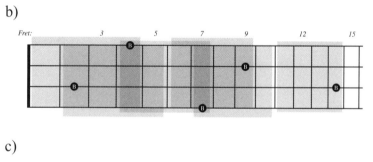

c)

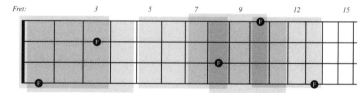

d)

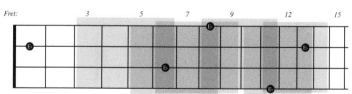

Quiz 23

1.

b)

c)

d)

e)

f)

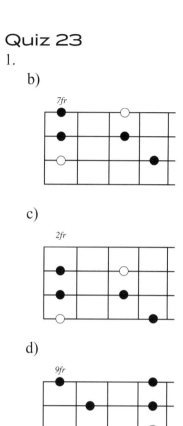

Quiz 24

1.

b)

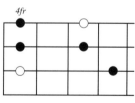

c)

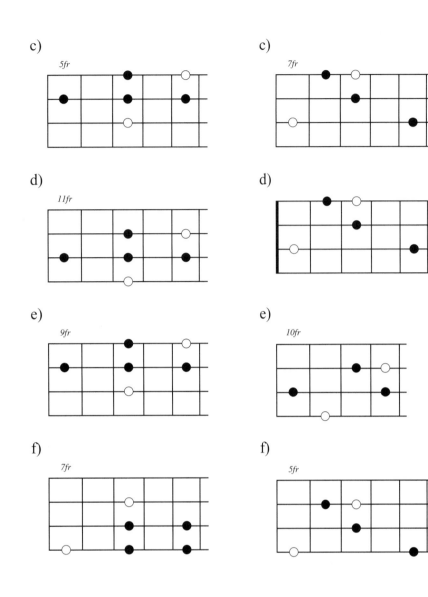

c)

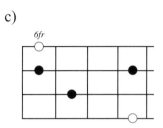

c)

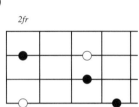

d)

d)

d)

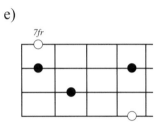

e)

e)

e)

f)

f)

f)

Quiz 25
1. 4

2. 1–3–5–7

3.
   a) A–C♯–E–G♯
   b) D–F♯–A–C♯
   c) B–D♯–F♯–A♯
   d) F–A–C–E

4.
   b)

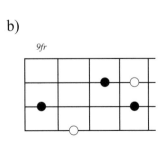

Quiz 26
1. 1–♭3–5–♭7

2.
   a) A–C–E–G
   b) D–F–A–C
   c) B–D–F♯–A
   d) F–A♭–C–E♭

3.
   b)

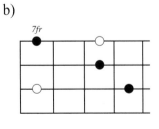

Quiz 27
1. 1–3–5–♭7

2.
   a) A–C♯–E–G
   b) D–F♯–A–C
   c) B–D♯–F♯–A
   d) F–A–C–E♭

3.
   b)

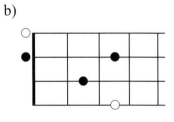